THE ART O
LIVING WE

THE ART OF LIVING WELL

Moral Experience and Virtue Ethics

Paul van Tongeren

Translated by Thomas Heij

BLOOMSBURY ACADEMIC
LONDON • NEW YORK • OXFORD • NEW DELHI • SYDNEY

BLOOMSBURY ACADEMIC
Bloomsbury Publishing Plc
50 Bedford Square, London, WC1B 3DP, UK
1385 Broadway, New York, NY 10018, USA

BLOOMSBURY, BLOOMSBURY ACADEMIC and the Diana logo are trademarks
of Bloomsbury Publishing Plc

First published in 2012 in the Netherlands, as Leven is een kunst, Copyright
Uitgeverij Klement, Zoetermeer.

First published in Great Britain 2020
Reprinted 2020 (three times)

Copyright © Bloomsbury Publishing Plc, 2020

Thomas Heij has asserted his right under the Copyright, Designs and Patents
Act, 1988, to be identified as Translator of this work.

Cover design by Charlotte Daniels
Cover image: Engraving of a Calville blanc d'hiver apple by
Pierre-Joseph Redoute. Published in Choix Des Plus Belles Fleurs, 1827
(© Nicoolay / Getty Images)

Bloomsbury Publishing Plc does not have any control over, or responsibility for,
any third-party websites referred to or in this book. All internet addresses given
in this book were correct at the time of going to press. The author and publisher
regret any inconvenience caused if addresses have changed or sites have ceased
to exist, but can accept no responsibility for any such changes.

A catalogue record for this book is available from the British Library.

A catalog record for this book is available from the Library of Congress.

ISBN: HB: 978-1-3500-1286-8
         PB: 978-1-3500-1287-5
         ePDF: 978-1-3500-1284-4
         eBook: 978-1-3500-1285-1

Typeset by RefineCatch Ltd, Bungay, Suffolk
Printed and bound in Great Britain

To find out more about our authors and books visit www.bloomsbury.com
and sign up for our newsletters.

CONTENTS

INTRODUCTION

Philosophy is about 'saving the phenomena'. This phrase, although coined by the ancient astronomers, was handed down through the ages as a conception of philosophy. Perhaps that is one of the reasons this expression is ascribed to Plato, being the first philosopher. 'Saving' is a translation of the Greek *sooidzein*, which can also mean 'to guard something', or 'to keep something from obscuration', as well as positively: 'to bring something to the fore'.

An artist only needs a couple of lines to draw a face and to show a person. Those who know the person that is drawn will instantly recognize him or her. You see something that you have not seen before, but nonetheless *recognize* it when you see it.

To show something with as few words as possible, to bring forth a certain meaning: that is the ideal to which philosophy aspires. But it seems philosophy is destined to use ever more words and above all to continually speak about itself, instead of just *being philosophy* and working as it should: to articulate what is meaningful and to put into words what it really has to say.

This book will inevitably elaborate, argue and discuss, and therefore I have tried to separate the different chapters by 'intermezzi': short passages that hopefully *show* some of the meaning that defines our lives as *human* lives. These short texts interrupt the argument of the 'main text'; however, they do relate to it. They always address the same two themes, which also determine the main text yet always remain in the background: human relations and our consciousness of our own temporality. They arise from practising ethics in a way that is clarified by and argued for in the main text. I have tried to resist explaining this relationship. Hopefully these texts speak for themselves, and will form a thread connecting all other passages.

Perhaps even these fragments end up using too many words. Perhaps philosophy has to become aphoristic to save phenomena. For that reason this books ends with a collection of aphorisms.

Nietzsche, master of philosophical aphorisms, called every philosophy – all great philosophy – 'something like involuntary and unnoticed memoirs', the actual heart of which is formed by the moral intentions of the author. The main text may already betray something about the author; the author is definitely (voluntarily or involuntarily) shown in the intermezzi – and even more so in the aphorisms at the end of this book. The reader can easily start there as well, before making up his or her mind as to whether or not he or she wants to further the acquaintance.

Art

When, in Homer's *Odyssey*, the Cyclops Polyphemus calls his one-eyed fellows for help after he has been blinded by Odysseus and has become powerless, his colleagues ask of him who it might have been that attacked him. He answers by repeating the name that Odysseus gave him: '*outis*', the Greek word for 'nobody'. Presumably the Cyclops was not familiar with the Greek language. His congeners apparently were, for they laughed at him and did not make any attempt to help him as, in his own words, he was being attacked by 'nobody'. Polyphemus must have felt tricked, in every sense of the word.

This must be the same feeling one has when trying to say something about art. Take for instance the literary art of Dutch writer Nescio (pseudonym of J.F. Grönloh). We have to make do with just a couple of stories, scarcely two hundred pages of prose poems written by him. The author answers every further question with only his name; this time in Latin: *nescio*, 'I don't know', or 'what do I know!'

Maybe there is still some hope – though that might be a misleading word. Maybe there is something to be found here. In the end even the Cyclops understood something: he understood he had been tricked and had lost. Not a very promising insight really, but an insight nonetheless. Perhaps Nescio also teaches us something, even if it is similarly lacking in promise.

The characters in Nescio's stories are in fact clear enough: Japi and the ones he exploits, Koekebakker and the other young titans, that is, the 'good kids' they were, before they grew up to be desperately bourgeois and reasonable gentlemen ('Except for Bavink, who went crazy'); and the little poet and his Dora. Who are these characters and what is it exactly that Nescio tries to say through them?

They are not easily characterized by their actions only; most of the time they don't do anything. If you want to describe them, it is probably best done by relating them to the three poles between which an area of tension exists that determines all the stories; three poles or positions: people, God and nature.

First of all, the people: mainly gentlemen, as reasonable and knowledgeable as they are despicable. Nescio and his characters turn away from them, or think themselves endlessly superior to them. Their know-how and their activism are directly opposed to the not-knowing of Nescio and the inertia of Japi and the other spongers, young titans and the little poet. For these 'kids' mainly do nothing: 'the truth is we did nothing but talk, smoke, drink, and read books'. 'The people', on the other hand, are always indulged in some activity or other; they slave away day by day, under the impression that it serves some goal. 'They just brood over religion, until God gathers them up [...] What they want is to struggle, to keep struggling along.' However much Nescio and his characters turn away from them, they ultimately find themselves in their midst.

With God they see two options: either 'the God that created Heaven and Earth', or 'the God of the Netherlands', the latter being only an extension of the people they turned their backs on. This second God is their projection: 'their dinner is their God', according to Bavink. It is 'the God your aunt believes in' or 'the God of all those who have no other option than to work or be bored'. The *other* God, the God of Heaven and Earth, is on the other side.

Opposite the scornful existence of the people stands the 'absolute transcendence of God'. This elevation is mainly shown by the fact that God needs nothing and therefore wants nothing: He doesn't reach for any goal, but is, on the contrary, completely aimless. For this reason He is, however, far removed too from our heroes (or rather: little heroes, i.e. the young titans). Indeed, they sometimes imagine themselves as sons of God – or even as God Himself – but soon enough they realize that this aimlessness was not made for them. 'Only God doesn't need anything.' And that is precisely the main difference between God and us. God knows there is no purpose, 'but not a single human being is able to constantly be fully aware of this'.

Inevitably, the nice guys become precisely the kind of person they don't want to be, and for as long as they are not, they, now and then, dream to be like the God they can never really be.

Only the third pole might be able to offer some form of consolation: nature. Nature is a middle position between the two other poles. On the one hand she resembles human beings: always in motion, always striving and trying to produce something. On the other hand she always does that in endlessness (the endlessness of infinite recurrence), the endlessness that robs every ambition of its goal and purpose. In one sense she resembles human beings: always fickle; in another this existence takes place in an endless cycle, making her similar to God's eternity. Well then: this nature, Nescio keeps telling us, is not only eternally recurring, but she *does not know* – the sea keeps rolling waves into the beach, 'the sea that complains, but doesn't know why'; 'the earth [...] from which the grain grows, which is green and turns yellow and is cut, and the high yarns stand on the yellow stubbles, and the earth does not know the least of it'; the air and the canal and the twilight and the light would always return, 'and they would know nothing about it'.

Could this not-knowing of nature perhaps be a clue? In between the busy and ambitious human pseudo-knowledge and the eternal, true knowledge of the divine purposelessness, stands nature, not knowing her own purposelessness – 'nescit'. So what Nescio and his characters ultimately aim for, is this: to become one with that nature, to resolve all ambition into purposelessness and, above all, to not know any more – for knowing only increases the pain, *scientia auget dolorem*.

As is known, Japi commits suicide by jumping off the Nijmegen railway bridge across the River Waal. Or rather: 'You couldn't call it jumping ... he just stepped off the bridge', 'his face turned to the north-east'. This was his way of becoming one with nature. As I said before: hopeful insights are not to be expected here.

Just as the Cyclops, we are left only with the way in which we were struck by those who conned us. For the Cyclops this means he remains, defeated, with a big trunk in his only eye. For us, on the other hand, it means we are left with some wonderful stories that have made an irreparable and indelible impression on us. Perhaps they have blinded us a little, but only in the same way the young titans were blinded: having looked into the sun for hours, and seen stars in their eyes for hours after. Such blindness simply comes with any injury we cherish.

I ETHICS AND MEANING

1 Life as art

Life is not an art as long as it is all about survival. Living usually goes automatically and naturally. In some cases it is difficult to survive, but not, I take it, for those who are reading this book. If life is about survival, we don't read books, but search for food or protection against violence instead. 'Erst kommt das Fressen, dann kommt die Moral' (['Food is the first thing, morals follow on'] Bertolt Brecht, *Die Dreigroschenoper*, 1928). It's only after our survival is more or less secured that the question arises *how* we should do it: live. Whoever seeks to survive, does not pose questions: he or she fights, (f)ea(s)ts and hides him- or herself. Only once that's taken care of, we can try to turn surviving into living; to get from feeding to eating, and from biology to art.

Art? Why 'art'? First, in the sense that 'art' refers to a certain *quality* of life. Life needs to be 'good', which means that it is more than 'just fine'. Of course, in asking ourselves how to live, we also want to know what rules we should follow and what we must do to prevent anything from going wrong. However, it ultimately comes down to something more than that – actually, not ultimately, but in the first place. For why indeed should we want to survive, and why should we want to live in a way that is 'right', if life itself is not worth anything? Therefore we are, first and foremost, interested in a life of quality, a life worth living.

Perhaps it's better to say we *should be* primarily interested in this kind of life, because *in fact* it is not everyone's first interest, not even for us – whose lives are safe. Why is that? How is it possible that we do understand the importance of the question 'why should we try to stay alive?', but nonetheless don't give it much thought? For one, because the answer to that question is not found easily – in theory, let alone in practice. It is not easy to live in such a way that it shows *why* we do it in the first place. And therefore we touch upon the second meaning of 'art': in the sense that it is a *skill*, a competence. For it is not easy to make something of life. It is quite an art, and one in which we do not always succeed. It can take a whole life to get to know the 'rules of the art'.

Third, 'art' also refers to *beauty*. The quality that life is all about, not only has to do with goodness, but also with 'beauty' – beauty in inverted commas, because it is a highly problematic word. Isn't beauty a matter of taste? What are we actually doing when we judge a work of art? We are only partly measuring it by general, predetermined standards. Not because art should be a matter of personal taste, but because art *creates* its own standards. What is made according to the (established) rules might indeed be very pretty and well made, but that does not yet make it art in the strong sense of the word. Many eighteenth-century paintings are, in their perfection, actually quite boring. Great art is not great because it perfectly realizes a rule we already know, but because it shows that which we didn't know yet. I mean 'beauty' in that sense: the beauty shown in art that is her own measure or standard. If someone asks us what we find beautiful about a work of art, there is certainly a lot one can say (see section 6), but eventually that's nothing more than saying 'Look! Listen!' A literary publisher once told me about the difficulties of commenting on manuscripts in a way that's valuable for the author: 'most people can write, but very often something is lacking: if I'm reading a book, I want to feel it *had to be* written, that it was *necessary*, or, to put it mildly: that it would be wrong to say that it might as well not have been written at all'. Something similar is true for the values we try to realize in life. We all know we could just as easily *not* have existed. It was a pure coincidence that those two people came together at that time under those conditions, resulting in my birth. But now that we are actually here, we try to live our lives in a such way that we cannot say in hindsight – so to speak – that it wouldn't have made a difference if we hadn't done so. We are interested in living a meaningful life, that is, a life that – just as a work of art – shows in itself whether it is succeeding.

It is with this art, the art of living well, that ethics might be able to help us. Sometimes it pretends to do even more than that; whenever it suggests that it not only gives an answer to the question of how to live our lives, but that it actually *is* the answer itself, or at least a necessary aspect of it. As Socrates said, the unexamined life is not worth living: *ho de anaxetastos bios ou biootos anthroopooi* (Plato, *Apology*, 38a). Even the lives of philosophers, however, are not always like works of art that show in themselves whether they are succeeding. There is more to the art of living well than philosophy. Yet, without self-examination, without a critical view on one's own life ('Is this all there is?') we will probably not succeed. Ethics is precisely this kind of examination. Ethical theories and concepts are tools for self-examination. Is that possible? Is a general theory capable of saying something about individual lives, about the quality of life and how to improve it? How does ethics do that?

2 Ethical cases

Ethicists like to make use of cases. One of the best-known examples is the famous 'trolley problem': a thought experiment first introduced by Philippa Foot, and then included countless times in textbooks. Imagine you are standing alongside a steeply descending railway, seeing an unmanned, runaway trolley car barrelling down. Down the tracks there is a switch. If you do nothing, the trolley car will take the track on the right. A little further down, you see a group of people on the track, unable to move, out of earshot and unaware of the approaching trolley car – if you decide to not do anything, they will be killed by it. You can, however, pull a lever, diverting the trolley car to the track on the left. On the left track you see only a single man, in the same conditions as the group on the right. Of course, the question is: what to do? Do nothing and let the group of people be killed by the trolley car or turn the switch, thereby actively taking part in killing the one man. If you think you have found an answer to that – whatever it is – the ethicist will show that you are wrong, by changing the case a little bit. Say, for instance, that there is only one single railway downwards, without any switches and levers; the same group of people remains further on the track, but this time there is a little bridge with a very fat person on it. If you push the fat person over the bridge onto the track, the trolley car will hit him and kill him, but be derailed as well, so you will have saved the group. You can, of course, jump onto the track yourself, but you are to small and skinny to have any effect on the trolley car. Again: what to do? What should one do?

There is something annoying about cases such as these. They not only force you to make very difficult choices, but present you with choices that are imaginary and in some way unreal. Therefore, in the end, they can be solved easily – that is, relatively easily. You just choose an ethical theory: if you decide to follow a consequentialist theory, it is clear you must make the choice that will have the best consequences. It might be a little difficult to grasp all the consequences, but you will figure it out. If you decide to follow a deontological approach, you will draw a different conclusion: killing someone without his consent is always and in any case wrong, end of story.

The case seems too extreme and the dilemma *therefore* difficult to solve. However, as soon as we try to translate it into an everyday situation, the dilemma grows even more difficult. In these cases the trolley car is replaced by your own actions: you are stressed by too much work; you feel disquieted and are unsure if that is a necessary condition for finishing a certain task, or rather a threshold; you leave a letter from a friend unanswered because you have already put him or her at distance and broken up in silence; you hide your feelings for another from your partner. There are plenty of examples. Time and again there is not just the one switch, but various possibilities to choose from. Besides, you have always passed several switches already: you have already taken up the tasks at hand, lived and organized your life in certain ways, put off your work; you could have started doing your work earlier, or ignored your passions for the other, etc. Even at this very moment there are plenty of different options for you to choose from: finally start doing your work or give up on the job; take some time off for a stroll; confess your feelings, hoping for forgiveness from your lover, or, on the other hand, keep everything to yourself, hoping it will remain a secret – and these are just the easy dilemmas. You could just as well fall in love with a third person, fall ill, travel abroad, go into therapy because you are burned out. On top of that, you are not 'an agent', as ethicists like to call it, but you are a particular, actual person with a specific background. You are someone that is very fond of his friends, or someone that longs to break free from all conventions; you have achieved something (or not yet); you have specific traits; you have just reached your thirties, or you are halfway into your forties, or a fifty-year-old man; perhaps you have children, and perhaps one of them got divorced; and so on, and so forth. Can ethics really mean something, even if the made-up cases are replaced by real life?

These examples were made up as well, but still they are more real than the trolley-car case. These are the kinds of examples we find in literary imagination. Take, for instance, the following two cases, that we can all relate to: living together with others, and our awareness that time passes by.

In the novel *Blindgangers* (Hermsen 2012), Dutch philosopher and novelist Joke Hermsen sketches a group of friends taking a weekend off for a trip to the country, far from the crowd. By the relative unity of time, place and action, the reader gets an intriguing glimpse of the lives and relations of seven characters: Iris and Johan, a couple with one daughter, divorced as a result of Johan's adultery, but now in an 'exemplary *post-divorce*', threatened, however, by the fact that Johan has sex with his daughter's girlfriend – something he tries to hide from Iris. Reindert is married to Medy, with two daughters, but lives together with Ella, who has a son from a previous marriage; they are in love with each other, but fail to establish a bearable relationship with Medy and both daughters. The relationship between Bas and Anna knows no adultery or break-up, but between the two they lack conversation and sex: they have nothing to say to each other, avoid any intimacy and seem to be kept together only because of their children. They both suffer from this situation, but seem to have found a modus vivendi or a way to make the suffering bearable. And then there is Det, who is an orphan, single and childless. Seven lives and a network of relationships. Even the relationships between them are not always simple and clear: they enjoy each other's company, but annoy each other as well; they try to have a cheerful weekend off, but they keep arguing amongst themselves; they support each other and let each other down. It is fictional, but a realistic situation that inevitably raises moral questions. Apparently there are many ways to mess things up: is one way better than the other? And what does 'better' mean in this case? Fewer problems, the least harm for the smallest amount of people? Healthier, happier? How much 'collateral damage' can happiness bear? Damage to yourself or to others? According to the famous first sentence of Tolstoy's *Anna Karenina* 'All happy families are alike; each unhappy family is unhappy in its own way.' But is there only one kind of happiness? Do the characters in Tolstoy's novel act wrongly? Could they do better? Are they unlucky? Can you make your own luck? Living together is an art in itself – can ethics say something about it or help us with it?

The beginning of the first part of Marcel Proust's monumental novel *À la recherche du temps perdu*, contains a passage on the young Proust longing for a goodnight kiss from his mother:

My sole consolation when I went upstairs for the night was that Mamma would come in and kiss me after I was in bed. But this good night lasted for so short a time, she went down again so soon, that the moment in which I heard her climb the stairs, and then caught the sound of her garden dress of blue muslin, from which hung little tassels of plaited straw, rustling along the double-doored corridor, was for me a moment of the utmost pain; for it heralded the moment which was to follow it, when she would have left me and gone downstairs again. So much so that I reached the point of hoping that this good night which I loved so much would come as late as possible, so as to prolong the time of respite during which Mamma would not yet have appeared.

Proust, vol. I, *Swann's Way, Combray*

Even in the language in which he expresses his memory, by elaborating and adding extra parentheses, it seems as if Proust is trying to delay the moment he longs for. He fears the moment he awaits so eagerly, for when it arrives, it will be the beginning of the end. After the goodnight kiss she will disappear. He is torn apart between desire and postponement; he cannot bear the delay of the moment he at the same time tries to keep at bay. Everyone is familiar with this phenomenon Proust sketches: that is why the second half of a holiday always feels a lot shorter than the first, or 'why life speeds up as you get older' (Draaisma 2006). Can ethics say something about these situations? They are all somehow connected to the 'quality of life', but in contrast to the trolley-car problem they are not about the question 'what shall I do?' Perhaps there are indeed some choices to be made, but the primary question seems to be of a different kind: how should one see and judge the situation? How did you become who you are, and how do your present actions shape your character? Is one way of acting better than the other? And what does 'better' mean in this case? Say, for instance, one way results in better health and more happiness, so we judge it to be better than other options, then what? Must we 'prescribe' or 'recommend' this course of action? Can someone become who he or she is not? And again: what does 'better' mean in this case? Can ethics say something about these questions? Can it be more than 'trolleyology'?

3 Facts and opinions

One way of claiming that ethics in regard to these 'personal matters' can say *nothing* is the following: ethics strives, just as any other philosophy, for real understanding and tries to make statements that are true. Well, we can only make true statements concerning an actual state of affairs.

However, the quality of life, the meaning of certain actions, the value of honesty and different kinds of love and friendship, they all exist in a way that differs from matters of fact – about them we can have only opinions. And, like taste, there is no debating opinions.

The distinction between facts and opinions is widely shared. When we read a newspaper article, we expect a clear distinction between a presentation of facts on the one hand, and the journalist's take on these facts (i.e. 'his or her' opinion) on the other. Our education system is keen on teaching us to make this distinction. Students are tested on their factual knowledge. Of course they need to learn how to formulate their opinions on them, but can these opinions in themselves be 'true' or 'false'? Is it possible for a teacher to approve or disapprove them?

In particular, when raising a child this distinction can become painfully clear. I myself remember trying to get my adolescent son to go for a walk or to a museum, and that whenever I told him it was good for him, he always had his answer ready: 'No, Dad, that's what *you think* is good, but that doesn't mean it *is* good!' An opinion is not a fact. Facts are fixed and must be acknowledged, but every opinion is subjective; why should one opinion be more true or valued than the other? He had learned his lessons at school very well, and not only at school. Once, when he had participated in a competition in which children had to make a video themselves, I attended the award ceremony. The winning video was a kind of documentary on the competition itself, in which the other participants and teachers were interviewed about the essentials of making a good film. The answers repeated the same chorus: it all comes down to following your own feelings, having your own vision, and putting your own opinion forward. My son had done the interviews.

The problem with this distinction between 'objective' facts and 'subjective' opinions becomes clear once you disagree with each other. How could I have convinced my son that my view is better than his (or how could he have convinced me)? Of course, I can try to explain why my proposal is good for him: 'Walking is healthy, it is a good diversion, you come across unexpected people and things; in a museum you learn how to look, can be moved by something of great beauty, or get annoyed by something you do not understand and thereby get to know yourself a little bit better, and so on.' But that does not help, because all it does is connect the activities that I recommended to him with other things *I* find important. He can just as easily keep repeating his answer: 'I understand *you think* all these things are important, but that does not *make them* important!' Because opinions are not facts, they cannot – it seems – be wrong either; at most, you can believe them wrong, but that is also just an opinion. What becomes clear now, is something paradoxical: on the one hand, an opinion (especially that of the other) is of no importance at all, because it is an opinion only and not a fact; on the other hand, however, one's (own) opinion is inviolable and indisputable.

If arguments are out of place with regard to opinions, discussions are in fact superfluous as well. My son was therefore often surprised that I kept trying to convince him, while we, according to him, just differed in opinion. Discussions on this were as futile and useless as all the discussions in the media or in parliament. Indeed: who has ever seen someone be convinced by the other in one of the daily discussions on the radio or on TV? At the end of these programmes, the different opinions are facing each other as much (if not more) as at the start. It is kind of strange when the presenter tells his listeners that he hopes the discussion was in any way helpful or valuable. For how could one learn anything from a discussion, if opinions cannot be argued since they can be 'only subjective' and therefore not true or false – after all, they are not facts!

By the way, sometimes my son also resorted to arguments. He said – perhaps just to get rid of his father's persistent nagging – that I should ask other people for their opinion, then I would discover that more people would agree with him than with me. Pollsters often suggest the same thing: that numbers matter. The same thing goes for some 'opinion-making' programmes, in which listeners are called upon to give their opinion via text message, telephone or email. At the end, the 'score' is announced. But what does it actually say, that most people have a certain opinion? If opinions cannot be true or false, they will not become so through being held by the majority. Or should we draw the cynical conclusion that, precisely because they cannot be true or false, their number is all that counts: the best opinion is the most popular opinion? But if most people regard a hamburger as the tastiest food, or find *The Great British Bake Off* (also popular in the Netherlands, as *Heel Holland Bakt*) the best TV programme, does that make it the case? Is an opinion more true to the extent it is more widespread, and is the most widespread opinion always the right one?

There is something strange about the distinction between facts and opinions. First, it seems to be logically wrong. Facts are the object of observations. The way you get to know a fact is that you find or register it. Opinions, however, are of a very different order: they are themselves a form of knowledge, but of another kind than determined or observed knowledge. An opinion is not a registration, but an interpretation, not an established fact, but an interpretation of … well, *of what* actually? If established knowledge concerns facts, what does an opinion relate to? What is the object of an interpretative opinion? Or, to present this point schematically: if we have to replace the opposition

fact vs opinion

by the double opposition:

observed knowledge vs interpretative opinion

of – on

facts – ?   ?   ?

then what should we write down in place of the question marks?

The second strange thing about the all-too-common distinction between facts and opinions, is that this seemingly descriptive distinction has an evaluative character. For we seem to be convinced: it's all about the facts. Opinions are subjective and, for that reason alone, less important. I suspect, however, that if we logically correct this distinction, this will also have important consequences for our relative evaluation of facts and opinions.

4 Meaning and quality

I think we should replace the question marks with 'meaning', or possibly 'value' or 'quality'. We can observe and register what is the case, but we have opinions *only* about its quality. We may count how many people have a certain opinion, but we then go on to interpret or form an opinion about the meaning of that fact. 'Interpreting' opposes 'observing' in the same way that 'meaning' opposes 'fact'. Ethics – and I think philosophy in general – is not about facts, but about meaning and about quality.

This means philosophy – as I understand it – can be clearly distinguished from science. Science tries to acquire universal knowledge about facts. Philosophy is concerned with the interpretation of their meaning. Ethics, as part of philosophy, focuses on the moral aspects of that meaning, on what we experience as good, great, right, meaningful or the contrary. But if those meanings and qualities do not exist as facts, what kind of 'knowledge' thereof can we have? What kind of cognitive pretensions can philosophy have? If we can 'only' have opinions about meaning, if there is no truth to be found here, does that not mean the failure of philosophy, and therefore of ethics? For what help can ethics be to the good life, if it is not through a kind of knowledge? What kind of knowledge can philosophy offer if it does not know any facts? Is philosophy perhaps only the initial stage of science, and is it time we leave that stage behind? Should those parts of philosophy that cannot become scientific perhaps acknowledge that they are meaningless or in any case do not provide universally valid knowledge?

Of course, in reality the distinction is not as simple as it appears to be. Philosophers often do scientific work and scientists do not escape interpreting. Furthermore, the meaning about which we form an opinion is always a *meaning of* something factual. The fact that the sun is shining evokes the meaning of beautiful weather – at least in my dark and cool part of the world in north-western Europe. The qualification 'terrible' belongs to the earthquake activities recorded by the seismograph in Haiti. Just as there are no meanings without facts, there are no facts without any meaning. All the same, the distinction between the two, even if it is schematic and abstract, can help to focus the problem. Therefore I will hold on to it for the time being and I ask the – philosophical – question what implications follow from this way in which we distinguish fact from meaning. This is a philosophical question because it, too, searches for a meaning: it asks what that distinction means.

I claim the following: if 'meaning' can only be the object of interpretative opinions, concerning which there is no truth possible, and thereby leaving no room for worthwhile discussion, then this would have dramatic consequences.

My argument for this claim has four steps:

(a) *Everything revolves around meaning.* This is a reversal of the popular opinion I quoted earlier. It is not all about facts, but about meaning. How could a fact be meaningful if we distinguish that fact from its meaning? Apart from these somewhat sophistic arguments, it can also be shown in other ways that human life is not about facts, but about meaning. The difference between humans and animals does not lie in facts, but in meaning. That humans 'eat' and animals 'feed' is not a difference in facts. Factual differences are at their best relative and changeable. In the circus you might see animals eating with a knife and fork and a napkin around their neck. The difference lies in the meaning of our 'food'. That is why we eat at set times (those who are hungry often look at their watch!), we tend not to eat alone, we measure our food and differentiate according to the time of the day, and so on. The same goes for the difference between humans 'making love' and animals 'mating'. The difference lies not in the facts. We pretty much all do the same. There is, however, an endless difference due to the meaning it has for us and the way in which that meaning is woven into the fabric of other meaningful things: love, loneliness, relationships, jealousy, desire, fantasies, expectations, etc. In human life, it is all about meaning.

(b) Still, though, meaning is far more important than facts (if we stick to that abstract distinction for now), it is only of facts that that we can acquire definite knowledge. *Regarding the meaning of something, we are fundamentally unsure.* It is also true that our lives are determined by all kinds of facts (the time of the clock, the rhythm of day and night, the presence or absence of others, etc.), but all these things cannot be separated from the network of meanings in which they are embedded. And each of these meanings is changeable and can be questioned. Night-time can change from a period of rest to a last chance to get something done. If someone kisses me, it is of importance not due to the touch of her lips on mine, but because of the meaning that it has for both of us. As to what specific meaning or significance it has, however, we can only guess. I think, or hope that it expresses affection, love and affirmation, but it could be a Judas kiss that betrays me. This uncertainty can never be totally removed. Of course, you can tell from further reactions and behaviour what was meant by that kiss. However, all forms of behaviour can be concealing, and can be interpreted in many ways. You can say in words what you wanted to express with the kiss, but even more than actions, words are unreliable.

This example of the kiss may be misleading: it suggests that all I am after is knowledge of the other person's intentions, of what meaning she attaches to her kiss. But in fact, the same uncertainty applies regardless of the other person: how do I know what my desire for her means? How do I know the meaning of the fact that the sun rises and sets, that seasons change, that many people live on this earth, that we sometimes collide with each other, that accidents scare us, that humankind has a long history that influences individual political interests and electoral considerations, that there are scientific institutions, that stores close at a certain time, and so on? Usually we do not worry about most of these things. We have more or less mutually agreed on the meaning of things: one must 'seize the day', 'we need each other', 'integrity is required', 'sciences advance and bring progress', and so on. These conventions, however, remain fundamentally changeable and therefore uncertain. The fact that we try to control this uncertainty about the meaning of our words, actions and experiences through agreements and conventions, however, does show something interesting.

(c) Apparently *the only way to make our uncertainty about meaning bearable is to seek confirmation from the other.* Sometimes we do this explicitly ('what do you think about the rise of populism?'), but usually implicitly: through all these forms of communication by which we share our experience of things with others – that is to say, present to another person for confirmation – but mainly through all kinds of habits in which a civilization more or less codifies the meaning of things. If you had to ask every person you meet what such an encounter means, it would drive you crazy. That is why we have the convention that teaches us to greet one another; to further avoid having to question what each particular meeting means, we greet according to a formula: 'Good morning!' But we do not greet everyone we come across. There seems to be something changing in society at this point: bus drivers notice that many people get on the bus without greeting them. For many people we encounter, it seems like we do not consider them as other persons, but as instruments. Is that true? Was the bus driver right who, after everyone had got on and he had closed the door, instead of driving away, took up his microphone to say that something horrible had happened: of the ten people who had just got on, only one had greeted him. Or is this not a matter of being right or wrong? Is it only a matter of subjective preference? One driver likes to be greeted; to another, it makes no difference.

(d) If opinions are nothing more than subjective preferences, there is no point debating them. Then we have to settle for 'tastes differ'. Perhaps we could then decide to greet that particular bus driver to remain on good terms with him or because we feel sorry for him if he feels ignored. This would, however, still remain a matter of 'feeling' and 'choosing', and one can only choose for oneself. It would leave us inevitably alone in our interpretation of the meaning of things we experience. This kind of isolation is, I think, unbearable.

To understand why that would be unbearable, imagine yourself living in a country whose language you do not understand. To do so is not only difficult; after a while it is even deadly. It starts with only small difficulties: you will have to put in a little bit more effort when asking for directions, shopping or trying to get help. But all these things remain possible. A cry for help, a repelling attitude, a photo of the hotel, a drawing of a loaf of bread and a finger pointing at a mouth: everyone will understand them anywhere. In other words, all requests and statements concerning matters of facts (distress, hunger) and the desire to change them remain possible, even if you do not understand the language. Conventions on the meaning of a greeting, of eating and drinking together, of appreciation or disapproval can still be learned in this situation. What is no longer possible, however, is to say something about what you think is beautiful or ugly, good or bad, meaningful or foolish, and why; in other words, to say something about meanings and qualities. And because or as long as this is impossible, we cannot stand such an alienating environment. You will start talking to yourself when there is no one around to share your interpretations with, and in the long run it will drive you mad. *We have an ineradicable need to show and share our interpretations of the meaning of things to others.* This need arises from, on the one hand, the uncertainty we feel about them, and, on the other, the desire for certainty: we want to know whether what we think or feel about our experiences is true. As long as conventions work there is nothing wrong, but as soon as they are no longer sufficient we feel the uncertainty that was kept at bay by these agreements and customs. In order to overcome this uncertainty, to gain certainty, we present our interpretation to others and ask them whether it is true. As soon as this is no longer possible, human life becomes impossible.

5 Aristotle

What I have described so far is actually an explanation of a famous passage from Aristotle's *Politics* (1252b28–1253a19). 'Politics' or 'political science' for Aristotle represents all of practical philosophy. This text is fundamental to what I propose in this book as ethics. Aristotle also starts by distinguishing between the good life and mere survival, and he states that politics finds its destination and legitimacy in the first:

> A complete community constituted out of several villages, once it reaches the limit of total self-sufficiency, practically speaking, is a city-state (*polis*). It comes to be for the sake of living, but it remains in existence for the sake of living well. That is why every city-state exists by nature (*physei*), since the first communities do. For the city-state is their end, and nature is an end [...] (1998: 3)

The self-sufficient polis is the ultimate goal, because it enables us to do what we ultimately desire: the good life, live in a valuable way. The polis is there to serve the good life, and the good life is desired for its own sake. The purpose of the polis is to enable the *praxis* of the good life. According to Aristotle, this is a political *praxis*; we shall see further on for what reason and why for Aristotle political theory is the highest practical discipline, which also includes ethics. In the remainder of the passage he explains what this political praxis consists of and why it brings human nature to completion:

> It is evident from these considerations, then, that a city-state is among the things that exist by nature, that a human being is by nature a political animal (*ho antroopos physei politikon dzooion*), and that anyone who is without a city-state, not by luck but by nature, is either a poor specimen or else superhuman. [...]
>
> It is also clear why a human being is more of a political animal than a bee or any other gregarious animal. Nature makes nothing pointlessly, as we say, and no animal has speech (*logos*) except a human being. A voice is a signifier of what is pleasant or painful, which is why it is also possessed by the other animals (for their nature goes this far: they not only perceive what is pleasant or painful but signify it to each other). But speech is for making clear what is beneficial or harmful, and hence also what is just or unjust. For it is peculiar to human beings, in comparison to the other animals, that they alone have perception of what is good or bad, just or unjust, and the rest. And it is community in these that makes a household and a city-state.
>
> (1998:4)

Just as I wrote earlier on the difference between eating and feeding, between lovemaking and mating, Aristotle refers to the difference between the speaking of humans and the buzzing of bees or the mooing of cows. This difference is in fact nothing but a difference in meaning. Humans are beings of meaning. In the field of meaning, according to Aristotle, moral quality is central: 'good and bad, just and unjust'. Along with Aristotle (and Plato and Socrates) we could classify that moral quality as 'justice'.

Moral meaning or moral quality is not only the most important thing in a human life, but also the most vulnerable and problematic. For it is not simply given, it is not a 'fact' and no one 'has' it or can 'register' it. We inevitably experience ourselves and the world in terms of 'good or bad, just or unjust' and the rest, but we never encounter justice 'objectively'; that is to say, justice always depends on our own interpretation. We always and inevitably perceive what matters to our lives from a certain perspective. And for this reason we need each other: the only way we can even begin to test our interpretation of meanings, the only way we can make them less personal and distorted by our contingent perspective (and again: this is important because meaning is what human life comes down to) is by presenting them to and discussing them with other human beings. The nature of meaning (so essential to human life) is such that we cannot escape discussing it with others – or else we would go mad, consumed by doubts or trapped inside our own illusions. According to Aristotle it is precisely this need for communication that makes us political beings.

People depend on each other, not just as 'beings of need' (as 'a bee or any other gregarious animal'), but as 'beings of meaning' as well; not only with regard to our 'means of existence', but with regard to our 'means of understanding' as well. In section 1 I wrote that if our 'survival' is more or less secured, the question arises why we actually want to live, of the meaning of life and the quality that our life should have. It now appears that this too had already been prompted by Aristotle: self-sufficiency with respect to our basic needs makes it possible to cultivate our desire for meaning; the assurance of our existence enables us to dedicate ourselves to the *praxis* of living well, which includes the *praxis* of understanding – or more accurately, of the attempt to establish a common understanding of meaning.

Now, have we made any progress regarding our initial questions: how (in ethics) to acquire knowledge about (moral) meaning and quality, how to say something about it, something more than just a subjective opinion? Wasn't the above nothing more than an argument for shared opinions, which might just as easily be called common illusions? For what reason does Aristotle connect meaning with *logos*, why do we – as beings of meaning – not simply look for the consensus of the herd? Why should a decent and dignified existence be an 'examined life', as Socrates stated (section 1)? Why do we desire to know if our own interpretations are correct, and how are we to find out whether they are? And what can 'correct' actually mean if it refers to a meaning that we cannot test 'objectively'? Is this not all very 'subjective'?

6 'Objective' and 'subjective'

By means of a few thought experiments I will try to show that knowledge does seem to be implied in our statements on moral meaning or quality (yes, even in our statements on aesthetic quality), and that these statements can in any case not simply be dismissed as 'subjective'; or better still, that we have to re-evaluate and define the meaning of the concepts 'subjective' and 'objective'.

Suppose you are the first to wake up and when you are reading the paper, your partner joins you for breakfast. You have just read that the president of some country (I was writing this down for the first time in February 2011, refering to the then president of Egypt, Mr Mubarak, but unfortunately there were many new examples since then and there will always be new examples) has caused chaos in Egypt his country to fight the insurgents and deliberately allowed militias to slaughter each other to prove that there can be no order and stability in the country without him. You tell this story to your partner adding your own opinion: 'What is happening there is a disgrace: sacrificing human lives in order to remain in power!' Now suppose your partner responds: 'Ah – you are not into that kind of thing? I like it actually, it's quite exciting!' You will probably look surprised, as if she did not understand what you were saying! After all, her answer seems inappropriate and unfitting. Your statement did not mean to express your own preference or aversion to certain practices, but a judgement about it; you did not want to express how you felt, but make a claim as to the meaning or worth of that practice. If she was to say 'I actually think it's smart, and maybe even the only way to take back control', then she would still not have agreed with you, but at least she would have been involved in the same 'language game'. Like you, she would have given an evaluation of the case. Her first reaction was a misunderstanding, because you wanted to discuss the matter, whereas she told you about her feelings. Apparently there is a difference between a judgement about a case, an 'object' on the one hand and the expression of a feeling, the self-expression of a 'subject' on the other. The first is 'objective' in a sense that the latter is not. And the first includes some sort of knowledge claim, while the latter does not.

This raises the question whether my 'objective' (i.e. 'object-oriented') judgement about the case can also be called 'objective' in another sense. I may have claimed not only to be expressing my emotions, but forming a judgement on the matter as well, but can I actually prove that? Can the verdict 'The president's actions are outrageous' be argued for in another way? Can I refute an opposing view with arguments? Can a value judgement be supported by arguments?

For a second thought experiment, we will pick an example from a field that seems even more 'subjective' than moral and political discussion – the domain of the aesthetic. We often assume that beauty and ugliness are matters of taste, and 'in matters of taste, there can be no disputes', because 'tastes differ'. Now, imagine the following situation. Your friend joins you for a visit to a museum, let's say to an exhibition of sculptures. You know from experience that both of you have your own pace and preferences, so you agree that you will meet each other in the restaurant in an hour. As you make your own way through the museum, you are suddenly struck by one of the statues – a female figure, for instance, crouching, one hand in front of her chest, the other leaning on her foot. You keep on looking at it for a while, walk around it to see it from all sides; if the attendant is gone for a moment, you cannot resist the temptation to touch it. You are deeply impressed by the statue. When you finally walk on, your eyes are drawn to the statue again and again, and when the hour has passed, you once again walk through the hall with the statue on your way to the restaurant. Your friend is already there, and as you sip your coffee you ask: 'Did you see that statue of the squatting woman? I loved it!' Suppose she says: 'That statue? But that's pure kitsch!' I guess that will affect you – though I'll leave aside whether your main fear is for her good taste or your own. More importantly, this incident shows us that something went wrong.

It is strange in a way: if aesthetic quality is a matter of taste or subjective preference, we can hardly say that something goes wrong when two people seem to have different opinions. Yet this confrontation makes us realize something is not right. Just look at what you are inclined to do: you will explain to your friend why the statue is so powerful, expressive, clever, well-balanced, exciting and so on. Or perhaps – if you are less sure of your own judgement – you will ask her how she knows or what makes her think it is kitsch. In other words, by describing the statue objectively, you try to show why one judgement is correct or more likely than the other.

I think the point is clear: if we tend to argue in the case of aesthetic judgements or, at least in some cases, if we exclude the possibility of opposing judgements being true and if we see a difference of opinion as a problem that needs to be resolved, then how much more clearly will this be the case when it comes to moral judgements! Again the question arises: we may like to argue for a certain opinion, but is that actually possible? Does it make sense to argue about the truth of a judgement that can never be 'proven' in the first place? For that seems to be the case with both aesthetic and moral judgements. After all, there are no 'objective facts' that can ever prove the correctness of a 'subjective judgement'.

In a sense, this is indeed the case: a judgement is an opinion about the meaning of a fact, and this meaning itself is not a fact that can be registered. It is exactly this distinction that forces us, however, to be careful in our conclusions. A third thought experiment: suppose I enter a lecture room full of students to give a lecture, and suppose I bring a big rack with me, covered by a large white cloth. The students cannot see what is underneath, but I tell them I have brought a painting with me and let them guess what kind of image it may be. They make estimated guesses on the basis of our study programme or of how well they know me. Once they have declared their suspicions, I remove the cloth and it turns out to be an empty frame, there is no image at all. I fooled the students and they probably feel cheated. They believed to be making a guess about an image, which then turned out not to exist at all. Since the 'object' did not exist, their assumptions about it became purely subjective guesses concerning an object that existed only in their subjective imagination – and that imagination turned out to be an illusion.

But instead suppose I had brought a painting with me, uncovered this time; suppose I had asked the students 'what is the aesthetic quality of this painting?' Again, they could have formed an opinion. But in this case I would not be able to do anything like what I did in the first: I cannot 'reveal' that there was no 'objective' aesthetic quality at all; I cannot do anything that would make the students feel deceived or show them that their opinions were nothing more than subjective illusions. And yet even in this second case there is no signified 'object' to their judgement – at least not as a demonstrable fact.

I think the difference between both situations is important: in the first case, the 'object' discussed was in fact 'externally accessible' as well. That is, apart from our own speaking and thinking about it, we could remove the canvas and just look, register. Due to this possibility, it also became possible to expose the opinions and assumptions as subjective illusions by showing there was no painting at all. In the second case, however, this further possibility does not exist: there is no external access to the 'object' of our judgement. The only access remaining is the opinion. For exactly this reason there can be no question of deceit or 'purely subjective' impression. If there is an external access to the object of knowledge, it is decisive for the correctness (or at least the 'relevance') of our statements and thus for the extent to which we succeed in transcending our purely subjective ideas: if our representations match the facts, we have 'objective knowledge'. However, if there is no such external access, because our statement concerns quality or meaning – something that does not exist as a fact – we must try to test our way of forming an opinion differently. We will not be able to achieve the kind of objectivity I mentioned earlier, but that does not mean that we should inevitably remain trapped in subjective illusions. We will have to look for another way, without testing our opinion against 'the facts'. But against what, then? Against other opinions! That cannot possibly provide us with the same certainty as 'factual knowledge'. But what can it provide?

7 Dissensus and consensus

Let's see what we have established so far: human life is all about meaning and quality. Both are fundamentally uncertain; they are not waiting somewhere to be found, they do not exist as 'facts' and cannot be 'objectively' registered through external access. Nevertheless, we are searching for some certainty about it, because without it we would be displaced in our world and alienated from our own lives. The community is the medium through which we create this desired certainty. In part, this happens through the conventions under which we hide our uncertainty. However, that is only one side of the matter. The other side is the one where conventions are not sufficient, but where we put them to the test; that is to say, where we check our current interpretations. If we limit ourselves to opinions on moral meanings (right and wrong, just and unjust, laudable or reprehensible, etc.), then we can name the former side, the conventions, that of etiquette. The other side, that of critical assessment, we then call ethics. The philosophical discipline of ethics can then be seen as a further enlargement of and elaboration on the way in which we all relate, to a greater or lesser extent, to that other side and by 'practising' ethics, that is to say questioning each other and ourselves when it comes to the correctness of our opinions on the moral quality of what we see, do and experience. But once again the question arises: can we determine the correctness of our opinions and moral judgements? No, but we can continually allow ourselves to question it. In this case it is not by confirmation (or falsification) through external access, but through doubt that we are protected from the illusion.

Within a community we present to each other our interpretations of the world. Not only do we greet *things* – as in Paul van Ostaijen's poem 'Marc groet 's morgens de dingen' ('Marc greets things in the morning') – but we greet each other and speak to each other in order to check if we still understand the world and each other: 'Good morning', that is to say: 'I know you, I know we share something'; 'Lovely weather, isn't it?' or 'What a great night we had!', that is: 'We see things in the same way, right?' Of course, before you know it these expressions are simply thrown about in social interactions, and often we have no specific intentions with them. But in these social lubricants meaningful action is hidden, helping us to retain our status as beings of meaning. We express our admiration, wonder or indignation to test whether we are right to see things in the way that we do. That's why we are constantly in conversation with each other.

Conversations like these presuppose a certain consensus and coherence. If we do not speak more or less the same language, we will not understand each other. A certain level of agreement is needed for us to be able to discover that which we disagree on. This consensus, however, is by no means absolute. On the contrary: if we agreed completely, we would stop speaking to each other. In our everyday communication we may hope for agreement and approval, but we also constantly anticipate potential disagreement: 'The weather isn't great, if you ask me', 'Actually, I didn't have such a good time last night'. The diversity of voices is vital for conversation, as long as they still understand each other. It is likely for this same reason that Aristotle sees the political community as the ultimate community, in which all other forms of coexistence reach their goal: smaller and earlier communities may well show too much consensus. This unanimity might be necessary for survival – in times of need, disagreement is dangerous – but in order to live *well*, a certain dissensus is just as important. Only through the plurality of what Aristotle calls the political community can the good life be realized. In being confronted by other views, we can no longer avoid the fundamental doubt about the correctness of our own opinion and, as reasonable beings, we must examine, with each other, the worth of these opinions. This community enables us – or even forces us – to scrutinize our doubt and share it in mutual conversation.

This is essentially what is to be shared in society: the doubt, uncertainty, not-knowing. Absolute certainty is only granted to the extremes between which humans exists (Aristotle wrote: 'either less than a man [...] or better than a man'): God and animals know no doubt; whereas humans know just about nothing else, and they therefore need others. Ethics is a helpful tool in this doubt. Therefore ethics is fundamentally subversive: it undermines the unanimity that would turn a society of people into a herd of animals (a herd that lives under the illusion that it is 'divine', that is, that it knows the absolute truth). Ethics casts doubt where there is too much unanimity. Ethics (and the same goes for philosophy in general) is impossible when we claim to know the one and only truth, when we live in absolute certainty.

Self-evident are the things you do not think about. To reflect on things therefore means to take away their self-evident character. This is one side of ethics: its questioning and, in a sense, destructive form. However, at the same time ethics encourages us not to stand still within this uncertainty. It tries to show how we can turn our doubts into something productive, how to look for answers to our questions: answers that can never be fully determined, that will be scrutinized by ethics itself once they start becoming 'self-evident', but that nevertheless help us progress.

8 Socrates and the beginning of ethics

This conception of ethics can be illustrated, again, by the actions of someone we usually place at the beginning of the history of (philosophical) ethics: Socrates (469–399 BC). In order to understand how and why ethics started with Socrates, we must first go back to pre-Socratic times. To find out why and when ethics was born, we will discuss the period in which it came to be, when, in a certain sense, there was no ethics yet.

Socrates lived in a time we now usually refer to as the 'Classical period' of Greek antiquity (between about 500 and 350 BC), preceded by the so-called 'Archaic' period (between about 800 and 500 BC) that which we can learn about through the works of Homer. In a way, ethics did not exist yet at that time. Did people lack concepts of good and evil? No, but they observed their lives in absolute and self-evident terms. This was possible because in such a society one's function and place in the social order was absolutely clear. A slave had to do whatever was expected of the slaves, a warrior of warriors, a king of kings and so on, and everyone knew what that meant. You might say there were no 'people' yet, only 'functions'. Nowadays, we see people, as it were, as actors who exist separately from the role they play. In the society I am sketching here (cf. MacIntyre 1966: Ch. 2, 1981: Chs 10 and 11), people coincided with their role or function. For that reason no one in such a society could ask how a person should live his life, one could only ask how a king, warrior and so forth, should act. The answer to that question was always clear and therefore ethics was superfluous and even impossible. Ethics exists in asking the question how we should live or act, and therefore presupposes that we do not already have the answer to this question.

Did such a society ever exist? No. It is a retrospective description of a period as if it once existed. It is a description of 'good old times', when everything was clear, made in a period in which everything is not so clear any more. In the works of Homer, who lived at the beginning of the Archaic Greek period, we also find, to a certain extent, a similar description of a period that was, again, already bygone. The same pattern can be recognized in our culture's Jewish roots: in the book of Genesis we see Adam and Eve initially living in Paradise, without a sense of good and evil – without ethics. Precisely when Adam and Eve stop automatically sticking to the rules and start practising ethics (start to gain knowledge of good and evil, by eating the forbidden fruit), they are expelled from Paradise. Yet another story told by people who questioned, about a time when no questions were to be asked yet.

Let us, for a moment, pretend that such a period did exist. Why would it have ceased to exist? Imagine that such a society goes into war and that the king is defeated and enslaved by the enemy. Now, if a king becomes a slave, someone has to swap one role for the other. Through wars, but also via trade and migration, as well as through technological progress, people discover that the way their own society works is not self-evident. And the moment you start to discover that things can be different from what you are used to, you are inevitably struck by the question of which is the best option. The moment our way of life is no longer taken for granted, we cannot help but ask ourselves what the best way of living is – how we should act in order to do the right thing.

Ethics consists in asking that question. We have seen this question arise, but something needs to happen to prevent its immediate removal. To prevent the question from being stillborn, a midwife is needed to make the birth succeed. Socrates, being the son of a midwife, called his own philosophical method a kind of midwifery: *maieutics*. In Socrates' actions we see what else is necessary in order to really create ethics. What he does is remove the two threats to ethics. Each comes down to the threat of making the question disappear. For this can be done in two ways: either by showing that there is no need to ask the question because we already know the answer; or by showing that there is no point in asking the question, because it is unanswerable. The first I call 'restoration', the second 'relativism'.

Socrates overcomes both of these threats through two questions he keeps asking in his dialogues: a question to clarify something (what do you mean?) and a question to test a given answer (is this right?). Interlocutors who think they know the answer – who, 'restoratively' refer to the past, to authorities or prevailing beliefs – are asked by Socrates what they mean, until they have to admit their ignorance. For example: justice is giving to everyone what you owe them. But if you borrowed a knife from someone, do you have to give it back if you know that the other person is going to do something terrible with it?

Socrates' most famous interlocutors, the sophists, represented the other threat, that of relativism. Sophists were itinerant teachers in rhetoric and eloquence. They claimed to know everything, or at least that they could teach you everything you might need to know – even when it comes to the good life or justice. Not because they knew the answer to every question, but because they knew there was no true answer. Since there is no true answer to the question of what makes a good life, according to the sophists one should not try to find the answer in the first place; it suffices to learn persuasion techniques that will enable you to get what you want. This claim is argued for in a relativistic way: we cannot say what a good life is, we can only indicate what someone *considers* to be a good life – and this differs per culture, period or person.

In the first book of Plato's *Politics* Thrasymachus is the sophist arguing for this relativistic view. There is no such thing as true justice, says Thrasymachus; instead, what is considered to be just is in fact determined by whoever is in power. Everyone seeks their own advantage, and the one who has power uses the concept of justice to subject others to his own interests. Rather than asking what justice actually is, one should therefore strive to be in charge of things or outsmart those in power. After Socrates clarifies this idea (by asking 'what do you mean?'), he asks his second question: 'Let's see if this is correct'. Imagine that someone in power can do whatever he or she likes, but is mistaken; in other words, say that someone wrongly believes something to be in his favour. The sophist must accept this possibility, but thereby undermines his own relativism. After all, if there is a difference between what you *think* is good for you and what is *actually* good for you, we cannot help but search for the latter and test our opinions for correctness.

Socrates does not have to prove that there is a true answer to the question of what is good for someone. It suffices to show that we cannot escape realizing that we can be mistaken. In doing so, he has shown that the question of what is truly good defeats any relativistic attempt to get rid of that question. That is enough to make ethics possible. Ethics is the asking of that question. And we all do ask that question every now and then. Ethics can help us by doing this more systematically and based in theory. In ethics, the question itself is of more importance than any answer. This does not alter the fact that we can only ask the question seriously if we are willing to look for an answer. That is to say: look for an answer, knowing we will never find a definitive answer.

Literature

Arendt, Hannah (2003), Responsibility and Judgement. New York: Schocken. Random House.

Aristotle (1998), *Politics*, trans. C.R.C. Reeve, Indianapolis, IN: Hackett.

Draaisma, Douwe (2001), *Waarom het leven sneller gaat als je ouder wordt* [*Why Life Speeds Up as You Get Older*], Groningen: Historische Uitgeverij.

Hermsen, Joke J. (2012), *Blindgangers*, Amsterdam: De Arbeiderspers.

MacIntyre, Alasdair (1966), *A Short History of Ethics*, New York: Macmillan.

MacIntyre, Alasdair (1981), *After Virtue, A Study in Moral Theory*, Notre Dame, IN: University of Notre Dame Press.

van Ostaijen, Paul (1925), 'Marc groet 's morgens de dingen' ['Marc Greets Things in the Morning']. Available online: https://www.poetryinternational. org/pi/poem/6645/auto/0/0/Paul-van-Ostaijen/MARC-GREETS-THINGS-IN-THE-MORNING/en/tile.

Plato, *Apology*.

Plato, *Politics*.

Proust, Marcel (1992), *In Search of Lost Time*, New York: Random House.

Attention

Attention is the attitude that causes a person not to look, reason or talk things away, but to let them be as they are. Something can come into being as a result of our attention. Attention creates the possibility of presence. And this presence is a very original truth, a condition for all further and derived truth: true statements, true love, higher truths and so on. And this original truth arises, happens or is created by our attention, that is to say: thanks to the attention evoked and aroused by the poet.

For this reason I'm intrigued by the poem 'January' by the Dutch poet Ed Leeflang:

Januari

Er huist een aandacht in de aarde
die zij niet aankan of niet zegt

Was zoveel schijndood voor je weggelegd
je zou doordrongen zijn van de bevroren trots,
waarin je wat zichzelf niet kennen dorst
ijziger koesterde, in ongeduld bewaarde.
   cf. Kouwenaar

January

There is attention in the earth
one she cannot hold or show

If you were granted such deathly pretence
you would be overtaken by the frozen pride,

in which you icily cherished, impatiently kept,
that which does not dare to know itself

In this poem it is not a person that pays attention to something, but the earth itself: 'there is attention in the earth'. There is no paying attention, nor arousing, evoking nor drawing. The attention is not 'given' by anyone. She does something by herself, or actually she does not do anything; she is just there.

It is not at once clear what 'she' refers to in the second line. In Dutch, both 'attention' and 'earth' are feminine words. Is the earth unable to hold the attention, or is it the other way around? It probably does not matter. If there is a subject belonging to this attention, it certainly is not a human being, but the earth; even the earth turns out to be powerless: she cannot hold, let alone show the attention. She neither arouses nor attracts attention, but is inhabited by it. The earth is the element in which attention is at home.

Just as the earth 'has' the attention, attention 'has' the earth. She herself cannot contain the earth, or express herself. While philosophers – rather overconfident – tend to think that our attention can make things happen, as if our attention constitutes the earth, this poem says that attention (not only *our* attention, but even the attention paid by earth herself) cannot hold the earth. The earth escapes from attention, not because by chance there is not attention paid to it, but because she is too big. Earth transcends the attention she harbours.

It is almost as if the poet himself doesn't know what to make of those first two lines, which are like an oracular saying: completely true, but incomprehensible, unintelligible. Incomprehensible because the earth with her attention seems to be self-sufficient, she does not need us; she keeps us out in the cold white silence of a winter landscape: 'January'. As an emergency measure the poet starts to speak about ourselves after the blank line, in a powerless attempt to understand something of what is being withdrawn.

The second stanza exudes a very different atmosphere: after the solemn and stately first two verses, in the following lines the pace suddenly increases. Anyone who reads these lines out loud will notice the tempo is only slowing down somewhat at the end. Perhaps because both the poet and the reader realize that this attempt to connect to the earth and her attention has failed and cannot succeed. The second stanza tries, as it were, to make that connection through a comparison. However, this comparison is counterfactual from the very beginning: 'if what(ever) that earth is granted *were* granted to you, then you *would* . . .'. But it does not lie in store for you.

But there has to be some kind of connection between the first and the second stanza. The poet binds them very clearly by the A B / B C C A rhyming scheme. Two completely different verses, that nevertheless refer to each other in various ways. Are they perhaps reversed counterparts?

The second stanza describes the silent attention of the earth as a deathly pretence: the apparent death of the winter landscape. The trees appear to be dead, but this turns out to be a false impression: whoever looks closely can already see plenty of buds of new life. The frozen and snowy earth's crust hides the spring that is soon to come.

The poet says of this apparent death, which is in fact a promising pregnancy: suppose the same goes for you. Suppose you were so full of life, what would you do, how would you be? Would you pay attention to what is concealed inside yourself?

The answer is shocking: you would not speak of attention at all. Instead you would be proud of it, you would cherish it and you would be impatiently preserving it. So there is a sharp contrast between the first and second stanza in content as well. The silence belonging to the winter landscape is transformed into frozen pride and icy preservation. The powerless and silent attention is opposed with an impatient and appropriating pride. The penultimate line accentuates this contrast by reminding us of what it is we cherish so icily and preserve so impatiently. Its description 'that which does not dare to know itself' echoes the inability to 'hold or show' as mentioned in the second line.

The passivity of the earth and her attention is opposed by our own activity and impatience. The earth's inability to 'hold or show' is opposed by our cherishing and preserving.

Perhaps only the poem can protect us – in our frozen pride, our icy preservation and our impatience – from turning the apparent death into a real death. That our ability to create is nothing more than to follow the logic of creation until it reaches its end in killing.

As another poet writes:

Van alle maken is doodmaken
Wel het volmaakste

Of all kinds of finishing, finishing someone
is perhaps most perfect

GERRIT KOUWENAAR, *Gedichten 1948–1978*, Amsterdam: Querido, 1982: 532

Perhaps only the poem can protect us from that. Of course, the poem is a creation itself. 'Poetry' is derived from the Greek word *poiein*, which means to make or to create. But poetry is a creation that prefers to sing the praises of its own failure. There are countless poems on that. To quote Kouwenaar once again:

Taal maakt nooit leven
Schrijf dat maar eens op

Leven is namelijk veel
Te onfeitelijk voor wie het beleeft

Language never creates life
Write that down for once

For life is way
Too unfeasible for those who live it

GERRIT KOUWENAAR, *100 Gedichten*, Amsterdam:
Querido, 1969: 74

Poetry, as a way of expressing the inexpressible, is inhabited by an attention it cannot hold.

II HERMENEUTICS AND EXPERIENCE

German philosophers Leonard Nelson and Gustav Heckmann developed a method for philosophical enquiry through conversations based upon the examples set by Socrates. These dialogues are determined by the asking of specific questions. First, one needs a starting question – for example the main question of Plato's *Politeia*, 'what is justice?'; or questions like 'do we always have to respect the opinions of others?', 'is authenticity sufficient for good leadership?', 'is patience a virtue, or a sign of weakness?' and 'is friendship always a virtue?' Second, the enquiry itself is done by asking questions, just as Socrates did. However, anyone who would try to only ask the questions that Socrates asks would be done very quickly. In addition to these questions, we also need hypotheses; besides the questions 'what do you mean?' or 'is this correct?', one also needs a direction to look for an answer – or again, a question: 'what do you think of the following?'

Although ethics is primarily concerned with the asking of questions, it is only possible to ask a question for someone who is willing to search for answers and to test the possible answers. In the previous chapter, we saw that the asking of ethical questions is both possible and necessary. That's all very well, but is ethics also able to provide some answers? Can ethics claim to offer knowledge about the good life? In this chapter I will try to answer this question. First I will discuss one of the most astute critics of the knowledge claims made by ethical theories (in section 1). Then I will show what kind of knowledge an ethical theory can develop, and that this happens in different ways because there are different types of ethical theories (in section 2). By elaborating on the themes 'happiness' (in section 3) and 'human dignity' (in section 4) I shall give examples of the kind of answers that are to be expected from a moral theory. Finally (in section 5) I reconnect that way of doing ethics with the things I wrote on examples in the first chapter. Those who are not interested in the methodological considerations in this chapter can, without any problems, skip the first two sections.

1 A critique on the philosophical pretensions of ethics

In his book *Ethics and the Limits of Philosophy* (1985) Bernard Williams expressed his critique on the pretensions of ethics. The central question in that book is: what is philosophy capable of with regard to Socrates' question 'how to live?' Can philosophy answer this question? Do you have to philosophize to answer that question? Williams is sceptical about this, not because ethical questions are unanswerable, but because philosophy is unable to help us in finding answers to these questions. However, Williams uses the term 'philosophy' in a very specific way: that of a theoretical foundation, justification or test of the answers given to Socrates' question.

Williams shows the inability of philosophers to provide an answer to the questions of Socrates, unless they themselves are guided by a certain answer. Generally speaking, we can distinguish two types of answers to that question, the two that determine both main types of ethical theories as they are usually distinguished. These are usually referred to as *teleology* and *deontology* and are associated with the names of Aristotle and Kant respectively. Teleological ethics starts with an understanding of the *telos* or purpose of human life or action and tries to reason from there how to act to realize that purpose. Deontological ethics, on the other hand, starts from an original obligation (*deon*), from which it then derives the rules of the right life. Of both forms of ethics, Williams shows that they only have a justifying power for whoever already agrees with presuppositions of the answer. That, as Aristotle says, leading a virtuous life is in our own best interest, will only be convincing for people who have been educated in such a way that they are interested in a virtuous life. That a certain kind of life is in your best interest cannot be proved except in a way that presupposes that you already share that perspective. There is no external access to the understanding of the moral goodness of virtuous life. Kant rightly states that it is rational for everyone (that is, that everyone has good reasons), from their own interest in freedom, to oblige others not to interfere. That does not, however, necessarily mean that everyone has good reasons to accept what others ask of him or her. The deontological theory says something about what someone would reasonably do if he were purely rational. But real people are never purely rational. You would have to be prepared already to take an impartial viewpoint to follow Kant, but that readiness is by no means self-evident for real people who, after all, always attach more importance to their own interests than those of others. A rational theory not only fails to bring about this willingness, but it cannot even provide a solid basis for it, that is to say: it cannot prove itself to someone who does not already acknowledge it.

We therefore have to start from moral beliefs that are in fact already given and not expect that philosophical ethics can lead us to a certain conviction. But, Williams then asks, is an ethical theory able to test our actual moral beliefs? His answer is once again sceptical and he underpins this scepticism in a discussion of two ethical theories that are known as the most important contemporary forms of teleological and deontological ethics: *utilitarianism* and *contractualism*.

Bernard Williams is famous for his ironic criticism of utilitarianism. Utilitarianism, he says, prescribes certain actions from the point of view of an impartial observer, who is omniscient, impersonal and abstract, 'but otherwise normal'. Of course, such a person does not actually exist. One must always have a motivation to act or to do something, and motives are always personal and relative. Just as we can't give up our personal involvement ourselves, we would not accept it if our loved ones treated us from a strictly impartial point of view. Judges and politicians must be impartial, but a mother should care more about her own child than about any other child; I expect from my doctor, too, that he acts in *my* interest and not in a way that would be best in general or that would most serve the public interest.

John Rawls's contractualism is criticized by Williams in a way that is similar to his criticism of Kant. According to Rawls, rules of justice should be drawn up in a rational discussion in which we hide our personal interests under a 'veil of ignorance'. However, according to Williams the outcome of this discussion shows that Rawls in fact starts from a certain – liberal – moral understanding of what a person is. That is not a problem in itself, but it is if the theory pretends to say something that would also apply to people who do not share the same prejudice already.

An impartial point of view to build an ethical theory on is impossible; anyone who still presupposes it is in fact concealing a well-defined intuition. Philosophy cannot provide us with compelling reasons for accepting one or the other intuition. Ethical theory cannot provide a foundation for answers to Socrates' question, and it cannot provide an ultimate test for our moral intuitions: not from 'outside' those intuitions, since from there they can never get inside; nor from 'inside' those intuitions, since then they will not be able to 'escape' them enough to test them. Yet this does not mean that philosophy can do nothing at all in relation to Socrates' question, or that ethics is only a matter of feeling. It is a question of determining what we mean by 'philosophy' and 'ethics'.

2 Hermeneutics of moral experience

The image of philosophy that emerges from Bernard Williams's criticism is derived from scientific rationality. Science is about an understanding of the world apart from our own place in it (see Chapter I.3). Williams makes it clear from the outset that his scepticism only concerns these pretentious philosophies, but not *every* form of ethics. He, too, believes that critical reflection on Socrates' question is indeed possible, but does not call this reflection 'ethical theory', but 'ethical thinking'. According to Williams, its aim is 'to help us form a world, that is our world, in which we can lead a social, cultural and personal life'. Williams's book can therefore be read as a plea for the rehabilitation of practical philosophy that helps us achieve this goal.

This practical philosophy of 'ethical thinking' can in my opinion, be characterized as *hermeneutic*, although Williams himself does not use this term. Throughout the book – and, as far as I know, in the rest of his work – the term 'hermeneutics' does not appear. Nevertheless: what he describes as an alternative to ethics, and does not want to call 'ethical theory', largely corresponds to what I want to call *hermeneutical ethics* or ethics as hermeneutics of moral experience. Williams puts it like this: 'There could be a way of doing moral philosophy that started from the ways in which we experience our ethical life. Such a philosophy would reflect on what we believe, feel, take for granted; the ways in which we confront obligations and recognize responsibility; the sentiments of guilt and shame. It would involve a phenomenology of the ethical life' (Williams 1985: 93). He immediately adds, however, that this might well be a good philosophy, but most likely would not yield an ethical theory. As I said before, I believe that such a 'phenomenology of moral life' can be regarded as hermeneutical ethics. The most important thing is that such an ethics understands its task as an explanation or interpretation. As we explain a poem, we can also try to interpret, so to speak, the text of our own moral experience. In the words of Williams, now supplemented by me: such an ethics wants to explain what we mean by 'what we believe, feel, take for granted (about what life is all about); by the ways in which we deal with obligations and acknowledge responsibilities; by feelings of guilt and shame' and so forth. To indicate what this ethics would mean, I will briefly elaborate on a number of characteristics.

First of all, such ethics also considers moral reality and the moral experience from which it departs as an interpretation. Just as the poem itself is an interpretation of meaning that the poet has 'heard', so too moral experience is not only an object of interpretation by ethics, but also interpretation by itself: the *interpretandum* is also an interpretation. This means that moral intuitions or feelings are not explained as 'facts' by this ethics, but interpreted and understood as interpretations. For example, sciences such as sociobiology, ethology or brain science may be able to discover facts about moral life and explain them evolutionarily or otherwise: cooperation, for example, will yield an evolutionary advantage; love, insofar as it is connected with sexuality, will have something to do with those parts of the brain that we have in common with other animal species, and so on. Nevertheless, feelings of love and hatred, of trust and community spirit also form an interpretation of ourselves and the people around us, and of the meaning they have for us; interpretations that must be explained in reflections on the difference between love and friendship, between the love you have for your partner and the love you feel for your children, or on the expectations that lie in trust, on when our trust is broken, and so forth. An ethical theory that ignores its own hermeneutical character might mistakenly believe that moral facts, interests for example, exist as neutral data. Such a theory denies that interests only become morally relevant through interpretation; that, for instance, needs only become rights through interpretation. Bernard Williams criticizes utilitarianism as such a naive denial of the hermeneutical nature of reality. If that ethical theory states that acting justly is what satisfies as many preferences as possible, it forgets that those preferences are not neutral things in the world, but interpretations, and it misinterprets them by failing to recognize this. An adequate practical philosophy must therefore first and foremost try to understand the interpretation offered by moral experience. Williams therefore says of 'ethical reflection' – which he distinguishes from 'ethical theory' – that it does not lead to 'ethical knowledge', but that it does produce 'understanding' (Williams 1985: 168).

Second, hermeneutical ethics acknowledges that there is no starting point for it other than the interpretations we have in moral experience. So moral experience is not something that should be put between brackets or concealed in a universalistic, rationalistic way. On the contrary: it should be the starting point for our explanations. The ethical theories criticized by Williams try to base certain moral prescriptions on as few presuppositions as possible. For example, they try to put in parentheses what one or the other finds important or valuable, and only assume that people all have interests, to search as neutrally as possible for a rule that can regulate the advocacy of those interests. Instead a hermeneutical ethics offers a reflection that tries to bring out, describe and explain 'our moral preconceptions' – i.e. the way in which we always understand ourselves, the other and the world, prior to explicit ethical theorization, in moral terms, in terms of values and meaning. The language of such ethics is not as neutral as possible, but tries to include one's moral engagement as much as possible. So-called 'thick' ethical concepts, such as deceit, promise, coarseness, courage, shame, etc. are not excluded, but are, on the contrary, essential. The fact that these concepts are always personal, that they cannot be separated from the ways in which people feel connected to them, is not an obstacle, but rather a necessary condition for the kind of practical philosophy that is presented here. Hermeneutics provocatively argues that prejudices do not obstruct our understanding, but make it possible. Just as we cannot explain a poem without considering that it appeals to us, we cannot engage in ethics without considering our moral commitment. Instead of trying to reach for a position that is as similar as possible to no specific, personal or individual position at all, we should rather adopt a *human* position. Or, as Williams puts it: 'to see the world from a human point of view is not an absurd thing for human beings to do' (Williams 1985: 118).

The choosing of ethical experience as a starting point brings a certain indeterminacy of the object of ethics. This is not a culpable vagueness but a deliberate attempt to escape strict delimitation. One cannot say what ethics is about without having already started with 'doing ethics'; your preconception of what is morally relevant will affect your answer. Williams speaks of 'all those things that are relevant to answering Socrates' question', the question 'how to live?' Any further delineation is only possible at the price of a certain circularity: morals are those matters that have moral relevance for the answer to that question. It is quite possible that these things differ from person to person, from group to group and from culture to culture – just as different people are touched by different works of art.

Nevertheless, my explanation of what is appealing to me may reveal to someone else something that he or she had not noticed before.

Third, if ethics can only start from moral experience, this means that ethical theories that pretend to start elsewhere ('outside') must also be, as it were, reread and interpreted as internal interpretations of moral experience as well. Such an approach thus allows or even obliges us to reread the history of philosophical ethics as a collection of interpretations of (aspects of) moral experience, as a series of hermeneutical designs. Aristotle, Kant, utilitarianism and Rawls can – after Williams's sceptical criticism – be rehabilitated as 'partial' interpretations of moral experience. To this end, we must apply an elementary hermeneutical rule: the rule that says that one can only understand a text by reconstructing the question to which it is an answer (Gadamer 1975: 355). If we do so with the different ethical theories, we shall see that it is an illusion to think that they only provide different answers to one and the same question. Kant, Aristotle, Mill and Rawls ask different questions, and they do so because they explain different aspects of the moral experience.

Utilitarianism (a) answers the question: which of the available options promises the most benefit, i.e. offers the best chance of satisfying the most of the desires of the greatest number of people involved? Utilitarianism therefore presupposes a given objective and a given number of possibilities for action. It will inevitably provide relative answers (which option offers a better chance than the other ones?), and it will interpret acting in a 'poetic' (in the sense of the Greek *poièesis*) way (as 'producing' satisfaction) and thus use efficiency as an important criterion. Contractualism (b) answers the question of which rules we should agree on. It therefore presupposes a situation that can be characterized as a problem of cooperation between parties with different interests. This question already anticipates an answer in terms of impartiality and accountability. The Kantian duty-based ethics (c) answers the question of whether we are allowed to do the thing we have already done or intend to do. This theory thus focuses on what we ourselves really do, i.e. on our intentions. It seeks a categorical judgement and thus not only presupposes a given law or criterion, but can also only derive this from a concept of human being from which every particularity is removed, that is: humans as purely rational beings. Lastly, virtue ethics (d) answers the question of how we can flourish optimally, and thus understands our actions not as *poiesis*, but as *praxis*. Like Kantian ethics, it is not interested in the instrumental, but in the intrinsic quality of an action, but now (unlike in duty-based ethics) not measured by a fundamental obligation, but by the extent to which happiness is realized in that action. *Praxis* is acting that is not so much the means to an end, but the way in which the end is realized. Virtue ethics therefore necessarily refers to human life as a practice, and makes itself dependent on either a metaphysical theory of human life or on socially, historically and culturally determined (and contingent) views about what this practice is all about.

Different ethical theories can thus be interpreted as an equal number of interpretations of different aspects of moral experience. This experience teaches us that (a) we sometimes have to choose and that we have to take into account the consequences of our choice; that (b) we are not alone and cannot ignore the appeal (and sometimes the physical power) of others; that (c) our conscience forces us to examine our intentions self-critically, and that (d) we experience the situations we are engaged in as well as life as a whole as determined by a destiny that does not depend on our decisions.

This brings me to a fourth point. Another characteristic of hermeneutical ethics is that it is not aimed at reducing the multiplicity of moral experience, but rather increasing its richness. Typical of traditional ethical systems is that they reduce morality to what is actually no more than a single aspect of it. In hermeneutical ethics, reflection should be the other way around: instead of cutting down a plethora of moral ideas and views, we should collect and express as many as possible. These views are very diverse: they cannot be categorized under one heading (like teleological or deontological). The diversity of moral views and motives mirrors the complexity of the traditions we are part of. Human life cannot be reduced to only one interpretation of it. This may sometimes be the tragedy of human beings, but it is certainly part of our greatness. Its interpretation, too, is an ethical undertaking in the sense that it makes us more at home (Greek: *ètheios, èthikos*) in these traditions and in our own diversity. If you learn to understand different ethical theories and moral experiences better, you will also get to know yourself better. Understanding includes always self-understanding (Gadamer 1976: 108). This brings us back to Bernard Williams, who interpreted ethics as the sum of all things relevant to answering Socrates' question. Although this question was formulated as 'how are we to live?', we know (see Chapter I.1) that there is only one answer: to examine our own life; since *ho de anexetastos bios ou biootos anthroopooi*, 'the unexamined life is no life for a human being' (Plato, *Apologia*, 38a).

Are we not stuck in descriptive ethics, a kind of ethics that gathers possibilities, but doesn't give direction or guide us, that cannot prescribe anything and therefore can't be normative? The answer is 'no', but this answer needs to be supplemented by a more detailed description of the nature of normativity that such ethics can claim to have.

Of course, hermeneutical ethics will not be normative in the way of ethics that pretends to be able to formulate and even establish universal prescriptions. Such prescriptions do not exist, at least not as something else than interpretations of moral experience. We therefore distance ourselves from so-called 'universal prescriptivism' (according to which moral judgements can become universal prescriptions) and from 'cognitivist realism' (according to which moral judgements are based on real, unambiguous and knowable qualities of actions). Yet this does not condemn us to a relativistic ethics that only describes factual (and context-related and therefore relative) moral judgements.

A hermeneutical interpretation of Kantian ethics may lose the categorical normativity that Kant himself ascribed to it, but as an interpretation of what we experience as conscience it does indeed present an obligation. After all, an interpretation of what conscience prescribes will have to do justice to the experience of that conscience, which somehow imposes itself on us. Every interpretation is, of course, fundamentally disputable; like the interpretation of conscience or other moral experiences: who knows exactly what his conscience says, what true happiness is, at what point involvement turns into partiality, and so on? But as it is with texts: the dispute between different interpretations is only possible for whoever wonders what the text – or in this case, moral experience – actually has to say. The assumption that the text – or the experience of conscience, the experience of life as pointed in a certain direction, the desire for happiness, the appeal others make to us, etc. – has something to say, is the basis of the normativity of hermeneutical ethics.

According to Hans-Georg Gadamer, the beginning of hermeneutics lies in the fact 'that something touches us' (*dass etwas uns anstosst*), that 'things' have something to say to us, even if they do so by remaining silent. For this reason art plays such an important role in Gadamer's theory of hermeneutics: 'a work of art that has touched us no longer leaves us the freedom to ignore it, or to decide autonomously whether we want something with it or not' (cf. Gadamer 1993: 220). What applies to the artwork ultimately applies to everything that appears in a human world, and certainly to moral phenomena. Everything that touches or addresses us poses the question of what exactly it has to say and what we should do with it.

Moreover, this beginning of hermeneutics contains, in addition to normativity, a certain universality. This universality is, however, not the kind of universality of unequivocal precepts, but that of a universal conversation between interpretations, between the continuous attempts to understand things. This conversation takes place both within our own tradition and between different traditions.

In the next sections I provide examples of such hermeneutical ethics in an attempt to interpret two key concepts in different ethical traditions: 'happiness' and 'human dignity'. The point is not to present an accurate account of what Aristotle, Kant and others have said about these concepts. Instead, I want to take them as representations of a specific moral experience. I will try to explain something of that moral experience, which has been expressed in those concepts and in the traditions of theorizing about them.

3 Happiness

Aristotle's ethics starts with determining the goal of our actions and lives. Aristotle calls this goal *eudaimonia*, usually translated as 'happiness'. What is the art of living well, life as art, other than the art of becoming happy? But how does one achieve that? And what is this 'happiness'? I regard 'happiness' as a concept referring to an experience, albeit a rather complicated one. I will try to explain something of this experience along four lines. Each of them is formulated as an antithesis: subjective versus objective, form versus content, descriptive versus normative, autonomous versus heteronomous. These antitheses are – I think – characteristic of the complicated nature of the experience we refer to as 'happiness'. We are not forced to choose one of the extremes, but happiness always encompasses both aspects – without removing the antithesis. Our conclusion must therefore be that happiness is a concept that contains a certain tension – and perhaps that is why happiness can never be fully reached.

3.1 Subjective versus objective

What does our experience tell us about the question of whether happiness is something subjective or something objective? Does happiness coincide with the subjective feeling of happiness, or can we have an objective understanding of happiness? As already mentioned, I do not think it is a matter of either-or, but both-and.

It would be foolish to call someone happy who does not feel happy. Anyone who has spoken to someone who is depressed, or has suffered from depression him- or herself, knows that happiness does not lie in objective circumstances, but in the experience of them. Everything can be fine, and yet you feel unhappy. It would not only be foolish, but almost an insult to call someone 'happy' who, despite all the circumstances, feels unhappy. The subjective feeling of happiness is a *necessary condition* for happiness.

More important and difficult than the question of whether a feeling of happiness is part of happiness, is the question of whether there is anything else to happiness apart from this feeling. Is the feeling of happiness more than just a necessary condition? Could it not even be a *sufficient condition* to speak of happiness? If that were so, the subjective feeling itself would at the same time be the objective content of happiness. It would mean that whoever *feels* happy, *is* happy. And that would mean that it would be impossible to (justifiably) say 'he or she feels happy, but actually he or she isn't happy at all' or 'I thought I was happy, but then discovered I was fooling myself'. I assume that we can make mistakes with regard to happiness too, and that there is something more to happiness than just a subjective feeling. I will get back to this point when discussing one of the other antitheses. Now, I would like to focus on a related subject.

There is, in fact, a very classic way in which people have tried to resolve this antithesis: identifying happiness with pleasure. I am referring to the *hedonistic* concept of happiness, as we find it, for example, in utilitarianism. According to utilitarianism, happiness is identical with pleasure; the objective meaning identical with the subjective feeling (although that subjective feeling can be objectified: you can measure more or less objectively how many people derive how much pleasure from something, and compare it with how many others lose how much pleasure by it). If happiness coincides with pleasure, one cannot truly make mistakes when it comes to happiness, since we usually do not doubt whether something feels pleasant or not: you are happy to the extent that you feel good (pleasure). The only possible mistake would be to take a certain pleasure for the ultimate pleasure. As soon as you discover an even greater pleasure, you know you were wrong – not to say that you were not truly happy, when you thought you were, but that you discovered that you could become even happier than you already were. Happiness then equals pleasure, but pleasure can be present to varying degrees. This hedonistic interpretation of happiness thus attributes a major role to subjective feelings of happiness – too big a role, I think. There are several problems with the hedonistic interpretation.

Whoever identifies happiness with pleasure, either excludes many significant experiences or stretches the notion of pleasure so much that it no longer means anything. Dutch writer Jeroen Brouwers once said 'I'm happy not to be happy', and Nietzsche writes: 'Man does not strive after happiness; only the English do that' (TI, Maxims and Arrows 12). Both can only say so if happiness is identified with pleasure – a certain kind of pleasure: rest and comfort. Both mean to say that this is not happiness yet, but that there are things more important than pleasure, such as creativity or power. If we were to say that they derive pleasure from creativity or power, and therefore they too are looking for pleasure, we would also say that pleasure can mean peace and convenience as well as restlessness and danger. In that case, however, the term 'pleasure' no longer says anything, and should be explained just as much as the term 'happiness'.

The second generation of utilitarians already realized that quantitative differences in pleasure alone are not enough to explain the difference between types of happiness. One cannot say that studying gives more or less pleasure than swimming, but one can say it is a different kind of pleasure. John Stuart Mill recognized a difference in quality – so much so that the lack of one pleasure can be worth more than another pleasure itself: 'It is better to be a human being dissatisfied than a pig satisfied; better to be Socrates dissatisfied than a fool satisfied.' Nevertheless, Mill maintained the equation 'happiness = pleasure', but he nuanced it by also recognizing qualitative differences between kinds of pleasure. I do not think his solution really works, because of the nature of pleasure and how we are to understand the differences in quality between various kinds of pleasure.

Here I draw inspiration from Aristotle. Aristotle explains (especially at the beginning of Book x of his *Ethics*) that the different qualities of pleasure are not to be found in pleasure itself, but in the activities that are pleasurable or result in pleasure. The difference between the pleasure of solving a complicated problem and the pleasure of licking an ice cream is not found in pleasure itself, but in the different activities. The quality of pleasure is derived from the quality of the action. Because gaining insight is a higher activity than eating ice creams, the pleasure of the first is a higher pleasure than the latter. It is said that the last words of Ludwig Wittgenstein, who suffered a lot and rarely laughed, were: 'Tell them I've had a wonderful life!' Why? Because he was able to devote his life to the quest for insight. What does that imply for the hedonistic interpretation of happiness? That defining happiness as pleasure does not help us. After all, we still don't know what happiness is, let alone what we have to do to be happy. In other words, pleasure is an *epiphenomenon*, something attached to, determined by and owing its quality to something else. Aristotle says that happiness depends on action. This 'something else' – action – is where happiness lies; a hedonistic interpretation of happiness says nothing at all on this topic. To put it yet another way: happiness is always pleasurable, but that does not mean that all forms of pleasure can be called 'happiness'.

3.2 Form versus content

Did we not too soon put the theory (of Aristotle) in the place of our experience, instead of using it for an explanation of that experience? Why do we actually speak of 'our' experience? Isn't there a plethora of different experiences of happiness? Can the very notion that happiness is nothing more than subjective feeling not do more justice to this diversity? The fact that different people experience happiness in very different things means that happiness is something completely different to different persons: one person finds it in a life of sensory delights, another in an ascetic devotion to knowledge. The fact that we call all these very different things happiness could be useful because – or insofar as – they have a number of formal characteristics in common. The thesis would be: happiness is determined by a number of formal characteristics, while its content may be totally different.

We can also rely on Aristotle for the identification of these formal characteristics. He mentions (in Book I of his *Nicomachean Ethics*) a number of them, of which I will highlight one. Happiness is a goal, and not just any goal, not a goal next to others, not a goal you could exchange for another one; but the ultimate goal. It is the name for the ultimate goal: all other goals (becoming rich, helping others, becoming famous, or anything else) are ultimately supportive and subordinate to the ultimate goal of becoming happy. This is bound up with the fact that happiness is an all-encompassing goal: a goal that is self-sufficient, that does not need anything else besides it, and that cannot even become bigger if something else is added. For example: one cannot say 'I want to be happy *and* rich'. The desire to become rich is rooted in the idea that it would make us happier than if we were only happy – which is obviously nonsense. If being rich is important to you, it will be a component of happiness.

These formal characteristics of happiness are important because they can serve as a test for the assessment of possible contents of happiness. It is obvious that we cannot be satisfied with formal characteristics only; every form also has a certain content. However, we do not yet know whether everyone can choose his own content, or whether there is an 'objective' content of happiness. But at least the possibilities can now be tested against these formal characteristics. If something cannot be regarded as the ultimate and all-encompassing goal, it can at best be a component of happiness. But what can be considered as such? Which 'content', which way of life can be said to need nothing else beside itself, that is: to be comprehensive and ultimate? Did we not – in citing Wittgenstein's last words – suggest too quickly that a life devoted to insight is the highest or only real happiness? Doesn't that contradict our own experience, which perhaps recognizes happiness even more in simple lives than in the biographies of great, tormented thinkers? Can ethics say anything about the content of happiness?

3.3 Descriptive versus normative

The problem with determining the content of happiness lies in the fact that it is a step that everyone today is very afraid to take: the step from descriptive to normative. As long as you describe – that is to say: represent what people actually fill in when they are asked what they think makes them 'happy' – nothing is wrong. However, as soon as you pretend to be able to judge whether they are right to say so, as soon as you start defining 'real' or 'authentic' happiness, you risk becoming a moralist or paternalist or another kind of pernicious '-ist'. So I'm taking a risk if I try to do so anyway.

Aristotle explicitly takes this step from descriptive to normative, or at least evaluative. He first conducts empirical research: the results lead to a three-way split: there are people who identify happiness with pleasure (as most of us do); there are those who identify it with successful and honourable activity; some finally find it in thinking and insight. He then shows that each of these identifications is clearly insufficient: we have already seen this with pleasure, but success and honour are not sufficient either: we do not only want to be honoured, but *rightly* honoured, and insight alone does not make one happy, if at the same time one cannot take care of oneself in practical and social life (Wittgenstein's life would probably not be an example of true happiness to Aristotle). This test leads him to the next step, in which he gives a content-based interpretation of happiness. I will present Aristotle's interpretation, but first try to give two arguments against the objection I mentioned in the previous section, against the fear of normativity.

First of all, we must once again be aware that normative here is not the same as prescriptive (see section 2 of this chapter). The point is now to formulate a concept of happiness that allows you to test and compare all kinds of opinions about happiness, so that we can say, for example, that the kind of happiness that is being presented to us in advertisements (for instance in the Dutch magazine called *Happinez*) is not yet real happiness. Such a concept is normative because it is evaluative, but at the same time leaves people free to make their own choices, even if they are deceived. You do not have to force someone to say he is wrong.

Second, we must remember what we concluded at the end of Chapter I: what goes for happiness, goes for truth. The latter does not exist either in the sense that it lies somewhere ready for us to be found: nobody possesses the truth. But it does exist in the sense that it enables us to critically examine every truth claim. In other words: as long as or because we can say 'this may be presented as truth, but is it really true?', truth exists. The same goes for happiness: as long as or because we can say 'this looks like happiness, but is it really?', we have an idea of what real happiness actually is. That means that I don't have to pretend to possess the truth, to know what real happiness is. I don't have to be dogmatic or fundamentalist to legitimately ask whether someone is right in what he or she considers to be happiness.

Against this background I will present Aristotle's concept of happiness and I will try to put it into contemporary words. According to Aristotle, happiness comes down to perfect self-realization (*psychès energeia kat' areten*). By this 'self', which must be realized, Aristotle refers to the 'essential self', that is to say, what makes a human being a human being, what distinguishes us from an animal, and that is, according to Aristotle, the *logos*. The realization of this self is done in at least four ways: (1) 'think' in such a way that you acquire real insight, (2) act in such a way that you rightly receive recognition, (3) feel in such a way that your feelings do not cloud your judgement and that they are appropriate. If you know how to realize all that, you will (4) take pleasure in it. A life that (5) is characterized by this as a whole (for 'one swallow does not a summer make'), we call successful or happy.

Perhaps we could update this as follows: happiness is (4) taking pleasure in (3) a fully developed sensibility, an emotional life that enables you to experience many feelings to the fullest and adequately; (2) acting and living in such a way that it establishes your connection with other people; a connection that exists on at least three levels (your most beloved, those with whom you work and live together in a society, and your fellow human beings) and will therefore manifest itself along three different lines as love, recognition and solidarity; in all of this being guided by values – opinions on what is important or worthwhile – of which you (1) are aware that you do not choose them, but that they impose themselves on you, in which you 'believe', and to which you dedicate yourself; values that 'truly' hold true, to which you truly seek and which you critically examine. (5) It will be clear that happiness only applies to a life as a whole and not to a single moment – and that it is an ideal, one that is not easily achieved.

3.4 Autonomous versus heteronomous

There is one last point in which I would like to follow Aristotle in his determination of happiness, a point that our experience often reminds us of, and that warns us against the illusion of all kinds of fantasies of social engineering in which our culture is in danger of losing itself: happiness is not entirely in our own hands. However much happiness is a moral concept for Aristotle (it is the basic principle of his ethics), and however much that concept also contains an encouragement to act and live in a certain way (his theory of happiness is the basis of his doctrine of virtues), he nevertheless acknowledges that you don't control everything. The later Stoics have a different view on this point. They say that everything you cannot do yourself, for which you are not responsible, is also irrelevant to happiness. Whether you are emperor or slave, whether you are rich or poor, sick or healthy – that does not matter for happiness; happiness is only found in the quality with which you embrace your destiny. For the Stoics, happiness only exists in virtuousness. Aristotle on the other hand recognizes that apart from virtue you also need some luck. We won't call someone who dies far too young, whose children fail or perish, or who happens to be the victim of wars or disasters a happy person! In part, we are indeed in control of happiness, but in other part we depend on others and circumstances.

Our *autonomy* is demonstrated by the fact that we can overcome or eliminate certain forms of heteronomy, such as a nicotine addiction, but our heteronomy is demonstrated by the fact that we cannot shake off *every* dependency. Apart from the role of fate or chance, there are at least two main reasons for this. First, heteronomy is inevitably implied in the fact that *relationships* are essential for a happy human life. We cannot do without each other, not only as beings with needs looking for satisfaction, but also as beings of meaning who are focused on quality, on meaningfulness, on happiness (cf. Chapter I.5). Therefore, happiness is always something that must 'succeed' between people and that you do not entirely control yourself. Relationships cannot be managed entirely autonomously. Not only do you not choose the one you love, but you are touched, affected, caught by someone. Moreover, you inevitably build a relationship together. You cannot give to those who can't receive. You cannot love the ones who can't be loved.

Second, we said that part of happiness is dedication to a certain value. This dedication implies that the value we dedicate ourselves to is not chosen autonomously by ourselves. If I can choose it myself, I can't really dedicate myself to it. I can critically examine a value that imposes itself, but even this critical examination is guided by a value that I have not chosen myself, for example: insight. This heteronomy, in my opinion, has two consequences for an adequate understanding of happiness: first that – as Aristotle acknowledges – it includes a bit of luck (whoever happens to fall in love with someone who cannot let herself be loved has bad luck and will not be happy); and second that, because of this, happiness (as Aristotle perhaps acknowledges too little) does not only consist in perfect activity, but also in a perfected passivity.

4 Human dignity

I am trying to give examples of hermeneutical ethics by explaining key concepts of ethics as interpretation of experiences, and to explain those experiences with the help of those key concepts. The first example, happiness, was in line with the ethics of antiquity, particularly Aristotle's; the second example, the idea that human beings have rights and that these rights are based on the individual dignity of each human being, is usually taken to be typical of modern ethical and political thinking. Its strongest philosophical elaboration is probably given in Kant's ethics. But even Kant doesn't provide a real foundation.

There is something paradoxical and annoying about human rights and human dignity. On the one hand, it is one of the most widely held beliefs of modern times, but on the other, it is one of the most vulnerable things we know. Our awareness that people have rights and dignity is another example of what I have referred to as a moral experience. Let us see if we can explain it in more detail, in such a way that we do justice to both its fundamental character and its vulnerability.

This is another example of how hermeneutical ethics can be 'normative' at the same time. However, it will now become another kind of example, because of the style of explanation and because this time I will not primarily be guided by a (Greek) philosophical theory, but by a myth from the (Judaeo-Christian) religious tradition. This way I can include the two main roots of our European cultural tradition in this presentation of hermeneutical ethics. Hermeneutical ethics is a kind of ethics that is aware of the fact that we can only get to know ourselves through the theories and stories in which we express ourselves, and that values the tradition in which we stand and understands this tradition as an ongoing conversation in which we ourselves must learn to participate.

4.1 Violating the inviolable

The ('inherent') human dignity is famously mentioned in the preamble of the Universal Declaration of Human Rights as the basis for the rights further specified. The Charter of Fundamental Rights of the European Union (in the preamble) mentions human dignity as an indivisible and universal value, and in its first title (Article I.1) states that this dignity is inviolable. At the same time, this same human dignity is repeatedly trampled underfoot in many parts of the world. When people are murdered, tortured, oppressed or trafficked, there is a clear violation of that dignity and the rights based on it. If Europe excludes people from other parts of the world, that may be reasonable in terms of all kinds of European and long-term interests, but it is certainly not an example of respecting the dignity of the refugee. Human dignity is evidently not only inviolable, but also constantly violated.

Perhaps one can object that this paradoxical formulation is misleading. After all, 'declarations' and 'charters' are typically normative. Human dignity *should not be* violated. Therefore, *actual* violations may be a practical, but not a logical contradiction. However, this does not alter the fact that it is strange that something so fundamental can at the same time so easily be ignored.

Moreover, what does it mean if we say that this dignity is 'basic' or 'fundamental'? Do we only mean to say that other things (other rights) are based upon it? Or do we at the same time say that this dignity is itself the most profound thing we can say about human beings; that is to say, that we cannot reach behind or beyond that? If so, does this not also imply that there is no ground on which this dignity is based? That it is therefore groundless? And does that not mean that this fundamental value is also an abyss?

But if there is no foundation for establishing human dignity, doesn't this establishing become very arbitrary? Isn't this exactly what Nietzsche reveals when he calls human dignity 'a phantom' to which especially metaphysicians who lost God and therefore began to believe all the more firmly in morality want to adhere? And if human dignity depends on the arbitrariness of the people who, more or less anxiously but always solemnly and universally, declare and affirm it, what is it actually worth?

Is this unsteady or absent ground perhaps one of the reasons why some still (or again) appeal to religion and see God as guarantor for the foundation for what they themselves cannot found? But does an appeal to a book free us from the arbitrariness? What is the point of saying that humans owe their dignity to God? Are we not exchanging our own arbitrariness with God's arbitrariness? And does this not still mean to those who do not believe: human arbitrariness? That a religious tradition says that God has given inviolable dignity to humans – isn't that another way to indicate that we are still dealing with a groundless explanation?

4.2 'Foundation'?

Some people see the formulation of the 1948 Universal Declaration as an enormous step forward compared to earlier declarations, such as the American Declaration of Independence of 1776, according to which 'certain unalienable Rights' were endowed to them 'by their Creator'. With the self-assured declaration by the United Nations, these rights would finally no longer have to derive their strength from an elusive will of God, and as a result they were supposed to be stronger than before.

In the same eighteenth century – in which the Americans still based their rights on God – the strongest secular interpretation of human dignity was given in Europe, by Immanuel Kant. He showed that humans have inviolable rights based on their rationality. Every foundation of rights or rules draws from rationality (after all, we want reasonable, rational arguments). Rationality itself cannot be founded on anything other than rationality itself. But this also implies that no motive going against rationality can ever be valid. And if that is the case, then rationality is inviolable. And so humans, as rational beings, are 'an end in themselves' and do not only have a (comparable and therefore relative) value, but an absolute 'dignity'. The Universal Declaration of Human Rights may well be viewed as the political implementation of Kantian philosophy, and therefore its practical culmination.

The importance of such a secular 'foundation' of human dignity is obvious. Whatever has dignity must be respected. However, as long as the moral imperative to respect human dignity and the rights that are based on it is itself based on the other's will, that imperative is heteronomous. Even if the other is God, the law He enacts is based on the earlier obligation to obey Him. Such a law thus remains conditional or hypothetical: *if* you want to or have to obey God, you will also have to obey His laws. But this law will not hold true for people who don't believe in God. 'If God is dead, then everything is permitted', Dostoyevsky suggests several times (in *The Brothers Karamazov*) in the conversations between Alyosha and his brothers Ivan and Dmitri. If there is no God, there is no morality – as far as morality exists only as a law of God. God as the foundation of morality is – as Nietzsche shows very clearly – ultimately an undermining of morality. Moreover, if there are any people who believe that God, as a ruler, watches over the observance of the commandment by which He has determined that humans have dignity and that it should not be violated, they will hardly benefit from it. The violations do not diminish, and the measures of this ruler do not seem to reveal themselves until the *eschaton*, at 'the end of time'.

4.3 Religious explanation

I believe that such an interpretation of the appeal to God does not do justice to what religious tradition provides: not a 'foundation' but an explanation. Although this explanation does not provide a foundation, it can provide support for whoever wants to affirm human dignity and for whoever wants to understand a little more about the vulnerability of this 'inviolable foundation'. The basis for this religious explanation we find in the first story of Creation, right at the beginning of the Bible. The first story of Creation is quite different from the second. In the latter (Gen. 2) God formed man of the dust of the ground and then breathed into his nostrils the breath of life. And when he feels very alone, God 'makes' him a woman out of his rib and brings her unto him (Gen. 2.22).

In the first story (Gen. 1), however, humans are completely made at once, in God's own image. This last thing has to do with human dignity. The fact that humans have such an inviolable dignity does not stem from the fact that they were created (after all, the same thing goes for all the other creatures), but that they were created 'in the image of God'. For the name of God refers to that which transcends all else. And if humans are created in the image of that incomparable, and therefore absolute value, then they themselves will have something of that.

Again: this is not a philosophical foundation, but a part of an explanation. We should not constantly test the story on the basis of epistemological (let alone empirical) criteria, but try to find out how people have tried to explain and understand their experience of the meaning of their own being through this story. The question is not whether, with the help of a story from a religious tradition, we can find proof of human dignity. Instead, it is all about understanding what they and we mean by this self-proclaimed dignity. After all, we have established that it is not at all easy to say what we mean by this belief in the inviolability of human dignity and human rights. The firmness with which we declare that this is the case does not cure the uncertainty about what it actually means. So it does not seem superfluous to explain our own conviction a little.

If we thus try to explain ourselves to ourselves, we will inevitably have to do so in conversation with our tradition. We are always part of certain tradition, whether we acknowledge it or not. A tradition can be likened to a conversation that has already started before we get involved. To make sure that what we say is relevant, we will have to listen to what has already been said. Those who start talking without first listening do not know the meaning of the words they are using. There are many interlocutors in the conversation that is human culture. One of them – by the many centuries it has spoken, a very important one – is the Bible, the basic book of Jewish and Christian monotheism. Let us therefore try to listen to what is expressed in this primal story of our tradition.

The fact that humans are created in God's image is not a minor aspect of the story. It is mentioned four times in a row, and it is also emphasized and explained. While the earlier created animals are all made 'after their kind', humans are created not 'after their own kind', but 'in our image, after our likeness' – that is, God's image and likeness. After the first two mentions of this likeness (in Gen. 1.26) it says humans must have 'dominion over' the other creatures, and after the second two mentions (Gen. 1.27) it says that humans were created as male and female. We may suspect that the likeness to God has something to do with the task of humans, and especially with this plurality in which humans are created, and that this task and plurality both have something to do with their dignity. I will elaborate on both aspects in the next two sections.

4.4 Dignity as a task

It is striking that the mentioning of God's intention to make human beings that resemble Him is immediately followed by the task that is given to them. 'Let them have dominion over the fish of the sea, and over the fowl of the air, and over the cattle, and over all the earth, and over every creeping thing that creepeth upon the earth' (Gen. 1.26). And God's actual creation of humans is immediately followed by the same command: 'God said unto them, Be fruitful, and multiply, and replenish the earth, and subdue it: and have dominion over the fish of the sea, and over the fowl of the air, and over every living thing that moveth upon the earth' (Gen. 1.28). Apparently our likeness to God is related to our mission. Being like God thus implies 'having dominion over the earth'. This is indeed not surprising: for the believer, God is the Lord of the world, so his likeness will be too.

Perhaps this is connected to another concept from the same tradition (a tradition that understands creation not only as a one-off act 'in the beginning' and *ex nihilo*, but also as a *creatio continua*), namely a continuous creation and taking care of it. According to this story, this care would have been (at least partly) entrusted or delegated to humans. Some contemporary voices question the notion of 'human dignity', especially the Kantian interpretation of it, because it would create a huge gap between humans and the rest of nature. In their view it would confirm anthropocentrism, which in its turn is held responsible for the unworthy treatment of animals and more generally for the destruction of the natural environment. Instead of going into this discussion any further, I would just like to point out here that the biblical story connects the human dignity with the task of taking care for the earth. This means that, according to this story, dignity is not in competition with, but rather in the service of the welfare of other creatures or the environment. We can even conclude that this human dignity only exists to the extent that it is fulfilled, in other words: to the extent that this task of taking care is actually taken up. Human dignity is not a licence for the unrestrained exploitation of nature, but a task to take care of it. To a certain extent (for the place of humans is not an original, but a derivative) this can be called anthropocentric; but this anthropocentrism is by no means an obstacle to a responsible treatment of our natural environment. On the contrary, it is the other side of our responsibility.

Particularly important to us is this: in this explanation, human dignity is not primarily the basis for a claim against others, but a reminder of our own task. It is not primarily an inviolable fact, but rather an assignment; not a non-destructible foundation, but an easily forgotten or neglected mission. The fact that humans have an 'inherent dignity' does not primarily mean that we are allowed or able to do something, but that we have something to do or should do something.

4.5 Relationality

Even more important to us is the second element we found in the story: as an image of God, humans do not appear as a singular being, but as 'man and woman'. How should we understand this? How can humans – plural – be the image of God? Isn't the God of monotheism the singular par excellence?

Saint Augustine was one of the first to develop a theology of Holy Trinity. Without doubt, he is a very important author when it comes to the connection between the Trinity and the creation of humans. Augustine also refers to Genesis 26 and 27 for this connection:

> For God said: 'Let us make man in our image and likeness,' and a little later it was said: 'And God made man in the image of God' [Gen. 1.26–27]. It would certainly be incorrect to say 'our,' because it is a plural number, if man were made according to the image of one person, whether of the Father, or the Son, or the Holy Spirit; but because he was made in the image of the Trinity it was, therefore, said: 'in our image.'
>
> **AUGUSTINE** 2002: 86

Augustine continues to explain that God is Father, Son and Holy Spirit, but not in a way that He only became Father and Holy Spirit after He had his Son. God was always the Trinity, and therefore always Father, Son and Holy Spirit. We must not be deceived by these metaphors: for men being a father and being a son are accidental characteristics – a man *can become* a father, but that does not necessarily happen. Fatherhood is therefore an accident. In relation to God, however, 'nothing can be said according to accident, because nothing accidental can happen to Him' (Augustine, Book 5).

It will be clear that we need to understand the metaphoric nature of this text. For example, the fact that there is a father and a son does not mean that God is a male. Nor is it about biological relations. The terms 'Father', 'Son' and 'Holy Spirit' are used to clarify something about the relational nature of God. Being a father is something you cannot do on your own. You are only father in relation to the child you 'have', you are only child because of and in relation your parents. Even God cannot be a Father without a Son. For the Holy Spirit this may seem less clear, but is even more true: the Holy Spirit is – theologically speaking – the personalized love with which Father and Son love each other and with which God loves His creation. By calling God 'Father' (and 'Son' and 'Holy Spirit') the religious awareness expresses that God is essentially, through and through, completely relational.

If humans are created in the image of this relational God, it means that humans are also thoroughly relational beings. However, the image is not an exact copy. While God contains the relationships in Himself, humans only know them with others. Hence, a relational God, who creates humans in his image, has not created one human being, but many. Not only have humans always had a certain relation to their creator, but they have also – as an image of this creator – always been related to each other.

What does this mean for human dignity? If humans have a dignity because they are created as an image of God, and if that 'being an image' means the indicated 'relationality', then we must conclude that it is precisely as relational beings that humans have the dignity that elevates them above the rest of creation, that assigns them tasks, responsibilities and rights, and that obliges other people and states to respect them and to enable and encourage them to carry out those tasks.

This means that this human dignity cannot be interpreted in an individualistic way – as it has been in the liberal Western tradition. It is true that each individual on his or her own has an integrity that should not be violated, but only because they all depend on each other. The African concept of *ubuntu*, which says that a person can only be a person through other persons, seems to express the idea of human dignity better than Western interpretations. This shows that dignity becomes a task in another sense, a task in which we are interdependent. With dignity comes the assignment to give each other with devotion and love the dignity that characterizes them.

If human dignity is a twofold task, and if, moreover, we have to rely on one another in order to carry out that task, it is hardly surprising that our dignity, however inviolable it may be declared, will in fact be a very vulnerable thing.

5 Experience?

The previous sections were both intended as examples of ethics as hermeneutics of moral experience. What was the role of moral experience in them? In both cases, it did not seem to be the thing that was explained. In the first case I took 'happiness' as the central concept from Aristotle's eudaimonistic ethics as a starting point and used his *Ethics* to explain that concept, even though this explanation always referred to our own experience of happiness. In the second case, the starting point for our investigation was again an ethical concept: human dignity. In the explanation of that concept, however, I emphasized not an ethical theory, but a text from a religious tradition. In both cases the hermeneutics was in fact an interpretation of philosophical or religious texts. So why do I speak of a hermeneutics of the *experience*, moral or otherwise?

In both cases experience did play an important role. In the elaboration of what we mean by 'happiness' I kept relying on an assumed experience of it. In explaining the concept of 'human dignity' I started from the experienced tension between the awareness that human dignity is fundamental and extremely vulnerable. I tried above all to do justice to that conflicting experience, more than to look for a philosophical foundation of dignity. However, any ethics will probably state the same: that it is about concepts based on experience; that in its theory it tries to connect to that experience and at the same time to test those experiences (or intuitions) by a theoretical elaboration of them. Since John Rawls this has been referred to as the 'reflective equilibrium'. Moreover, experience and theory can never be sharply distinguished from each other: our theories contain content from our experience and our experiences are partly formed by theories. Ethics as hermeneutics of moral experience doesn't do anything other than what every ethic does, although a hermeneutic ethics may emphasize this link with experience more strongly and – above all – acknowledges that the concepts, theories and texts with which it works are themselves interpretations of experiences.

Perhaps we can clarify the role of experience in a hermeneutic ethics if we take concrete experiences as a starting point. Let's return to the examples from Chapter I. The literary texts I drew them from are already interpretations of these experiences themselves. What could an ethical interpretation of them consist of? What do we actually mean when we speak of 'experiences'? And is this truly about 'moral' experiences? What is 'moral' about the experience of more or less successful love, or of time passing by? Can experiences be the object of explanation at all? Is there no reason why I borrowed the examples from texts? Isn't it always *texts* that are the subject of hermeneutics? Isn't an experience quite different from a text?

5.1 Experiences are not facts

Experiences are to be distinguished from what people actually feel or their thoughts on what they feel. 'Experience' isn't something that simply 'is' there, as a fact, but something we 'do' ourselves. In the word 'experience' we should try to hear the verb. 'Experience' as I use it, belongs to what we saw in Chapter I about meaning. Experience is the awareness of meaning that at the same time presents and withdraws itself. So it is about 'being aware' or 'noticing' meaning, and therefore about something other than 'registering' pleasure or pain. The so-called gut feelings – or feelings we can only express in terms of 'I just find this good, beautiful, nice, tasty, etc.' – are at most a first and most primitive form of what may be called 'experience'. As long as they are not 'worked up' to a sense of meaning, they remain mute facts. In experience, however, facts lose their muteness, and are brought to speak. Then they say something, it turns out they have something to say. But they hide what they have to say at the same time. Characteristic of an experience is that the meaning that presents itself partly remains a promise of meaning. Experiences in this sense need to be interpreted, appropriated and (to that end) shared. That is why we tell each other about our experiences; not because we know what they have to say, but because we don't know exactly (or completely) yet. Experience stands for the receptiveness to meaning and the ability to deal with potential meaning that presents and withdraws itself.

The experiences of fictional characters in the novels I mentioned in the first chapter (I.2) are not the same as what they feel. If they experience impatience and anxiety, desire and fear, friendship, love, loyalty and infidelity, that is because something more happens than what they feel at a particular moment. The fact that they experience something means that they come across something that has meaning. When Iris gets angry when she discovers that Johan has an affair with their daughter's girlfriend, it is more than a physiological process, and more than just anger – even more than an expression of jealousy or of a difference of opinion about what a 'post-marriage' actually means. It also shows how personal relationships are intertwined with views on the need for intergenerational divisions. These dividing lines form an element of the structure of meaning we live in. However, we do not immediately know what this structure actually means. Any loss of trust raises the question of what 'loyalty' actually means and what 'the future' is when we make a promise that extends over a period of time we do not yet know. Little Marcel was confronted with conflicting desires: he wanted to postpone the fulfilment of his desire. His experience thereof not only consists in the simultaneity of opposing feelings: pain and pleasure from one and the same thing, namely the arrival of the mother. But his experience is also the confrontation with a certain meaning that at the same time hides itself: in this case an interpretation of what it means that everything passes in time.

Since experience – as has been said – is a discovery of some meaning, and since that meaning is showing and concealing itself at the same time, it is something else than what can be registered by some 'empirical' sciences and instead asks for an interpretation. That is to say: for a hermeneutics that is not by accident but essentially connected with experience.

5.2 What makes experiences moral?

What makes an experience moral? How can we speak of 'moral experiences' in relation to the earlier given examples? The answer is to understand 'morality' in a very broad sense: morality encompasses everything insofar as it damages or contributes to what makes a life good or worth living. Here we are reminded of the indefinite nature of what

Bernard Williams called 'ethics': all that is relevant to answering Socrates' question 'how are we to live?'. We cannot decide in advance what does or does not belong to morality, because we have no source other than our own experience. Any demarcation is arbitrary, even by those that say that morality only relates to what we are obliged to do to others, while ethics relates to the good life. Our relationships with other people are part of life, of which we wonder how to lead it in a good and worthwhile way. The principles for our judgement of what does and does not belong to the moral domain, we can also only learn from experience itself. And the principles we think we know can be challenged by that experience.

It is for good reason that Williams investigates the case of Paul Gauguin: the painter who left his wife and children to try his luck on Tahiti. Instead of simply morally condemning him, Williams looks for what this course of life can show us about moral meaning, in this case something about 'moral luck'. For wouldn't we judge Gauguin's actions differently if they hadn't contributed to the artistic form he found precisely on Tahiti and by his way of living there? Yet this does not mean that principles and criteria do not play any role in the judgement of someone's actions; even less that it does not matter whether or not you are faithful to your marriage vow or live up to your responsibility for your children. But these principles and obligations appear to be themselves to be in need of interpretation when we are confronted with concrete experiences.

5.3 Experiences and texts

How should we interpret our experiences? How can we treat experiences as if they were texts? The answer consists of three elements. First, experiences have always been formed by texts. Lovers express their love for each other in words they know from stories, films and songs. Our experiences of fidelity and infidelity, love and being in love, loneliness and security, adventure and familiarity, promise and guilt, desire and fulfilment, postponement and satisfaction, are all shaped by the books we have read, the stories we have heard or seen – not only the texts that we have read ourselves. The culture we live in and the way our society is organized are also partly determined and formed by texts. Even people that have never read the Bible are shaped by the stories that originate from it; the same goes for other great texts, films and even news items.

News increasingly consists of telling stories: of eyewitnesses, of victims, of journalists. And who would dare to say that we can still experience the events in the world without the narrative structuring we have received through those stories?

Second, experiences themselves are – at least partly – structured as texts. Paul Ricoeur (1991) characterizes a text as an emancipation or becoming autonomous in three ways. In contrast to speech, a text is set free from the speaker (an author is him- or herself a reader of the text as well), from references to actual reality (a text can address other events than the events that caused it to be), and from a specific audience (a text can be read by anyone). Of course, experiences are of a different kind from texts. And yet the same applies for experiences: we do not entirely own them; they do not completely belong to ourselves. Because our experiences are always already shaped by texts, they always stay at a certain distance. Our experiences are not already our own in a way that would make their appropriation superfluous. Moreover, they have a meaning that goes beyond their specific cause. This is most obviously shown in very strong experiences: experiencing serious crime is shocking because it shows a general boundary, precisely because it is crossed then and there; a relationship that is experienced as 'real love' shows a criterion that has a more general validity and thus transcends this specific relationship. Experiences have – through the meanings they show us – a bearing that is not limited to me. Remember the experience in the museum I described earlier (Chapter I.6), the need we feel to share our experiences with others; or something we all experience now and then: that our experiences are changed by the interpretation of others. Who is able to separate the experience of a memory evoked by a seemingly unconnected sensory sensation from Proust's famous description of the madeleine biscuit dipped into a cup of tea?

Third, the explanation of experiences is largely done by using texts. Proust's monumental novel is itself an attempt to explain the experiences that are presented in it. It is a way of looking back on the time that seems past and lost. In her novella about the siege of Leningrad in the Second World War, Russian writer Lidiya Ginzburg notes that people in the besieged city eagerly read Tolstoy's *War and Peace*, in order to discover what they themselves actually experienced. This instantly tells us what happens in an interpretation: by interpreting we become familiar with the meaning that at the same time came to us and withdrew itself from us. Anyone living in the surrounded city will experience something meaningful; but what it is exactly that they experience is at the same time withdrawn. By reading texts you try to familiarize yourself with what was already happening in your own experience; you try to appropriate what you experience yourself but did not yet understand' or at least not fully understand. This means that an interpretation is always aimed at an understanding in the first person singular. While description can be given in the neutral third person (one can explain why someone writes a text about a certain event at a certain moment), interpretation always focus on an understanding that must be performed by and for the subject itself. Hermeneutics is always focused on self-knowledge, and therefore corresponds well with the question of Socrates that I have quoted a few times already.

Literature

Aristotle (1975), *Ethica Nicomachea*, trans. H. Rackham, Cambridge, MA/ London: Loeb Classical Library.

Augustine (2002), *On the Trinity*, Cambridge: Cambridge University Press.

Gadamer, H.-G. (1975), *Wahrheit und Methode: Grundzüge einer philosophischen Hermeneutik*, Tübingen: Mohr.

Gadamer, H.-G. (1976), 'Hermeneutik als praktische Philosophie', in *Vernunft im Zeitalter der Wissenschaft*, 78–109, Frankfurt: Suhrkamp.

Gadamer, H.-G. (1993), 'Die Universalität des hermeneutischen Problems', in *Gesammelte Werke Bd. 2, Hermeneutik II*, 219–31, Tübingen: Mohr.

Nietzsche, Friedrich (1990), Twilight of the Idols (TI) (transl. R.J. Hollingdale) London: Penguin. (Original: *Götzendämmerung*. in: *Kritische Studienausgabe in 15 banden*, Berlin/München: DTV 1988, Band 6).

Plato (1826), 'Apologia Sookratous', in I. Bekker (ed.), *Platonis Scripta Graece Omnia*, 273–366, London 1826.

Ricoeur, Paul (1991), 'What Is a Text?' in *A Ricoeur Reader: Reflection and Imagination by Paul Ricoeur*, ed. Mario J. Valdés, Toronto: University of Toronto Presse.

Tongeren, Paul van (1994a), 'Moral Philosophy as a Hermeneutics of Moral Experience', *International Philosophical Quarterly*, 34(2): 199–214.

Tongeren, Paul van (1994b), 'The Relation of Narrativity and Hermeneutics to an Adequate Practical Ethic', *Ethical Perspectives*, 1(2): 57–70.

Tongeren, Paul van (1996), 'Ethics, Tradition and Hermeneutics', *Ethical Perspectives*, 3(4): 175–83.

Tongeren, Paul van (2000), 'Ethics, Tradition and Hermeneutics', in D. De Stexhe and J. Verstraeten (eds), *Matter of Breath: Foundations for Professional Ethics*, 199–32, Leuven: Peeters.

Tongeren, Paul van (2011), 'Ethics and the Limits of Philosophy', in Andrew Wiercinski (ed.), *Gadamer's Hermeneutics and the Art of Conversation*, Series

International Studies in Hermeneutics and Phenomenology, vol. 2, 531–46, Berlin: Lit Verlag.

Tongeren, Paul van (2013), 'Natural Law, Human Dignity and Catholic Social Teaching', *Religion, State & Society*, 41(2): 152–63.

Williams, Bernard (1981), 'Moral Luck', in *Moral Luck: Philosophical Papers 1973–1980*, 20–39, Cambridge: Cambridge University Press.

Williams, Bernard (2006), *Ethics and the Limits of Philosophy*, Abingdon: Routledge [first publ. 1985, Fontana Press].

Relations

In the Netherlands almost everyone is familiar with the so-called 'Loesje' campaign: small posters with witty texts, signed with a girl's name 'Loesje'. A while ago I saw one with the following text:

Je *wordt* al geboren, je *wordt* al begraven;
waarom zou je ook nog *worden* geleefd.

We slip into this world, we slip out of it;
Why should we let life slip away as well.

Nicely put, as usual with Loesje, although in this case I also felt a certain hesitation. Not that I would argue that we should just let our lives slip by. But it suggests that it would be better if we were to take it into our own hands. On the other hand, I believe we must take seriously the impossibility of taking the beginning and the end of our life in our own hands, and that this impossibility also has an important consequence for life between birth and death.

I am born by the help of others, and others bury me. The beginning and end of our lives are marked by a profound passivity that connects us fundamentally with others, that entwines us in relationships with others.

Although this seems obvious, we tend to forget it. This has to do with the history of Western European culture, and especially that of philosophy, or more broadly: that of knowing. At the dawn of modern times, important things happened in the human pursuit of knowledge. To mention one: in search of knowledge it was discovered that we first have to be able to determine whether the knowledge we *think* we have is *real* knowledge, and not an opinion, illusion or superstition.

Everyone probably knows Descartes's solution: he tried to doubt everything to see if there was anything left he could not doubt. And it turned out the only thing that could not be called into question was doubt itself: if I doubt whether I really doubt, then I know one thing for sure, namely that I doubt. We usually quote the famous *cogito, ergo sum*, 'I think, therefore I am', but in fact this is preceded by *dubito, ergo cogito*, 'I doubt, so I think'.

But *dubito, cogito* and *sum*, that is all first person singular: the only thing I know is, according to Descartes, that *I* know that *I* think. And just as it is still a long way to come from this beginning of certain knowledge to science about the world, so it is a long and difficult way that must lead from this 'I' to a 'we'. How do I know *you* think? Because you look the same way as I do when you do it? Because you say you think? These are all things that reach me through my senses; who says they don't deceive me? Descartes's great discovery may provide us an unshakable certainty, but it also makes him terribly lonely.

This is once again proven if we look at the philosophers who have been thinking about society since that time. They came up with the idea of the so-called 'social contract'. According to this idea, society arises when individuals – lonely individuals – make agreements with each other. They enter, so to speak, into a treaty and devise measures that force them to abide by that treaty. Well conceived, but however useful and fruitful this way of thinking may have been, it is not obvious.

It is by no means self-evident that society is created by a choice made by lonely individuals. Were these individuals not borne by their mothers? Did they lack brothers and sisters, did they not have any relatives? Didn't they have friends, allies, trading partners long before they decided to draw up a treaty? Didn't they have to feel *related* to other people to even get the idea of such a treaty?

As real children of modernity, as replicas of Baron Münchhausen, we would prefer not only to decide on every form of community ourselves, but also determine our own beginning; we would like to create our own origin. And we are increasingly trying to manage our own end as well. We cannot bear the fact that we are not in control of our own beginning and ending. Perhaps this insufferableness has something to do with our – typically modern – desire to sustain ourselves? But wouldn't the secret of beginning and ending become more bearable if we acknowledge the fact that others took care for us when we were born, and that we will be cared for by others after we die? Before 'I' was there, I was already part of the community of my parents and their family and friends; when 'I' am no longer there, in a sense, I will still be there: in the community of my friends, my children and their friends.

Well, if we in this way emerge from a community and reintegrate into a community, then it is probably not so strange to understand the part in between in terms of community or relations as well. A variation on the Loesje poster I started with could be: 'You are already being born from others, you are already buried by others, why should you think you can live all by yourself?'

Of course, we have all kinds of relationships that presuppose our own existence: for example, you have to be someone to be a creditor or debtor, a customer or seller, a pupil or teacher, a patient or doctor, and so on. But the person we are – or have become, or are becoming (for who can say that he or she has already finished becoming a person?) – is only created by another kind of relationship than customer–supplier or doctor–patient or whatever. And that other kind of relation is not on a level with the other ones; it does not even precede them in time, but *realizes itself in* all these other relations. In the relation between a teacher and a pupil, a doctor and a patient, a politician and a citizen, there is something else than the functionality of these relations. By 'functionality' I mean the reason why people enter into such a relation: you go to a shopkeeper to buy something, to a teacher to learn something, and so on. In these functional relations something else has to take place to make these relations into *human* relations. And this other something is itself something relational.

To be a person, I have to be known and recognized as the one I am; I have to be loved for who I am and someone has to take care of me. By the food someone gets, he or she stays alive, but by the love with which he or she gets it, he or she becomes a person. Someone who grows up without love, is violated in his or her humanity. By the medical treatment that someone receives, his or her body stays healthy – if all goes well. But medical treatments also constitute or disfigure a personality, because they are provided with more or less care and because the patient is or is not recognized as a person. The dedication of a teacher to the pupil not only makes the teaching more effective, it also makes the pupil a human being that is welcome in this world. The teacher not only earns money through the lessons he or she gives, but also becomes human by the extent to which he or she is recognized as a person by the pupil – or is affected by not being recognized.

People are not what they are before they enter into relations of recognition and care with each other: one becomes a person because of the way in which and the extent to which he or she is recognized and loved as a human being.

A human being is a creature not only born by another, buried by others, but also in between the two a human being through the love and recognition of others. That doesn't take away the fact that you have to do something to gain it; Loesje is right about that.

III VIRTUE AND THE ART OF LIVING WELL

Human life cannot be captured in only one interpretation of it, and ethical theories are different interpretations of what this life is all about. Hence, it is important to try to think about morality from several perspectives. Nevertheless: however much the previous chapter emphasized this importance of diversity of perspectives, each author has his own preferences and limitations. This chapter is about the leading perspective in this book: virtue ethics. Why virtue ethics?

Ethics is a form of practical philosophy. This not only means that it *deals with* praxis, but also that it *thinks in terms of* and *for the benefit of* praxis. To realize the latter, we will probably have to do something more than just help interpret what people experience. Although this is not unimportant, the practice of life requires more than just interpretation and insight.

'Of course, insight is also a step in the direction of practice. The quote from Socrates' defense speech, cited several times already (*ho de anexetastos bios ou biootos anthropooi*: 'the unexamined life is no life for a human being') suggests that self-examination is at least a necessary precondition for a human life, perhaps it was even a sufficient condition for Socrates.

That it is a necessary precondition we can understand in the light of what we have seen in Chapter I (from I.4 onwards): as beings of meaning we cannot do anything else but present to each other our own interpretation of meanings we perceive. Friendship and love, for example, are undoubtedly strong experiences of meaning, and therefore they require interpretation. Intense or complicated relationships can even confuse us so much that the question for interpretation and insight explicitly arises: what is going on with me; why can't I forget him or her? Other experiences only become necessary to interpret because we explicitly focus on them. So we read in Augustine's *Confessions*: 'What then is time? If no one asks me, I know what it is. If I wish to explain it to him who asks, I do not know.'

Insight and understanding of what you experience at least makes you a little more at home in your own life; that has everything to do with ethics. The Greek word *èthos* originally meant a hare's form. A 'form' is what we call the nest a hare 'inhabits'; it is not a hole in the ground (like rabbits have it), but in high grass. The hare creates his form by turning around at high speed for a while and thereby shapes the grass, as it were, in the form of its (rolled up) body. Just as a hare turns the grass into a home by turning around in it, so we shape our own life into a home (and protect ourselves against alienation and loneliness) by the interpretation and exchanging of meanings in the middle of which we live, and thus appropriate them. Hans-Georg Gadamer (1976: 108) rightly calls hermeneutics practical philosophy, because explanation is always self-explanatory: whoever learns to understand him- or herself better in that sense becomes more 'ethical' and more 'at home'.

Only an intellectualist like Socrates could think that knowledge would not only be a necessary, but even a sufficient, precondition. If our desires guide us automatically to good things, we need nothing but knowledge of the good to move in the right direction. But do we not sometimes act against our better judgement? And do we not have multiple and different, perhaps even opposite desires? The examples in Chapter I speak for themselves: Proust let the young Marcel say he almost wished that the goodnight kiss he so longed for would be postponed as long as possible; the characters from *Blindgangers* want to find each other and at the same time distance themselves from each other, be honest and not hurt each other, be faithful and follow their hearts. Conflicts everywhere. Is it only insight and understanding that can save them from it? Shouldn't an ethics do more to help them? Can it do more; can it help?

As I said before, this book seeks this help especially in virtue ethics. On the one hand, I immediately admit that with this, a certain one-sidedness is given. On the other hand, there are various reasons to think that virtue ethics offers more opportunities on this point than other ethical theories. In a brief summary of this form of ethics, I will focus on the characteristics that, in my opinion, make it more promising in terms of practical implication, or at least less overconfident (section 1). In my account of virtue ethics, I will mainly follow the classical, Aristotelian tradition. Nowadays this tradition is more in vogue, among others in the form of the very popular art of living. I will therefore discuss the extent to which the latter is indeed closely related to virtue ethics, but subsequently show that it is also distinguished from it in an important respect (section 2). By showing the difference, I will finally address a part of virtue ethics that does not yet seem to receive much attention in this current revival of its tradition (section 3).

1 Virtue ethics

In a sense, all kinds of ethics try to express what is good and what we should do; all kinds of ethics try to establish this knowledge of the moral good. The same goes for Aristotelian virtue ethics. In short, it considers happiness as the good, it calls the action required for that purpose an act from virtue and it underpins it in a theory of human nature. 'Happiness' has already been discussed in the previous chapter (II.3). In this chapter I will focus more extensively on the concept of 'virtue'. The foundation of this ethics in 'nature' (and the discussion about the extent to which the Aristotelian views on the order and dynamics of nature and especially the nature of humans are still tenable in the light of contemporary philosophical and scientific insights) will be discussed in more detail in Chapter VI. Without going into further detail, we can say that this ethics – unlike most modern ethical theories – states that morality is not at odds with our natural desires, but that in fact it is closely related to them. Morality is not about limiting and restraining our natural desires, but it tries to cultivate, refine and educate them. Aristotelian virtue ethics is an ethical theory in line with human desires. It is therefore also important to know what we actually desire, in what happiness actually exists, in order to know what to do.

However, moral problems do not only arise from our ignorance about what we are to do, but also and above all that we do not succeed in doing what we know is good. There can be several reasons for this. It can mean that there are several things to be done that are not easily reconciled. I already recalled what the examples in Chapter I showed at this point: the desire to postpone the fulfilment of a craving. Love sometimes requires restrictions that seem to go against love. These kinds of problems ultimately refer to a tragic character of human action, to which I will return in the last section of this chapter.

The fact that we often do not do what we know (or think) we ought to do, however, also and above all arises from that fact that our motives are not directly shaped by insights. Knowing that our natural environment suffers greatly from our use of fossil fuels does not take away my desire to travel quickly and comfortably. Even though I know that 'patience is a virtue', it doesn't make me any less unhappy when I'm waiting at the lift or in a queue. My awareness that I should not accept every invitation does not take away the seductive power of those invitations. My motives to act in this way or that are certainly not only determined by my knowledge, let alone by my knowledge of moral values and duties. Only gradually and via intermediaries can knowledge shape my desire and my motives.

That is what virtue ethics focuses on. It does not question what we – here and now – should do (and certainly not whether what we do or intend to do is lawful), but rather how we can train ourselves to become more who we 'actually' are, to be more focused on what we 'actually' desire. (There is a problem in this repeated word 'actually' that I will discuss in Chapter VI; for now it remains in scare quotes.) Working on who and what you actually are, 'becoming who you are', 'self-realization' happens by shaping your character, the sum of your attitudes. For that reason virtue ethics is not so much about actions as about attitudes. According to Aristotle, virtue is an attitude, a disposition. Aristotle calls it a *hexis*, *habitus* in Latin, *habit* in English. These translations show the importance of attitudes for our actions: the more they become a permanent trait, the more important they become. A habit is not only characteristic for the way in which a person has already acted, but it also, inasmuch as it determines an attitude, makes us prone to chose or act in a certain way in the future. Social scientists may argue about what has the biggest impact on our actions, character traits or contexts of an action, but the fact that traits have some influence seems evident. We not only recognize character by the way people act, but also anticipate their actions on the basis of them – even though these expectations usually are wrong.

This has to do with something else that plays a role in the fact that we often don't do what we know we should. For that 'knowledge' is not simply given. I 'know' my ecological footprint is bigger than the earth can bear, but I don't 'see' my footprint when I'm travelling, or planning a trip, or looking at all those nice pictures in a travel guide. My actions are largely determined by things I experience; that is, the things that I perceive. But the way I perceive them is shaped by my own traits or the attitude I have and determines who I am. One who has practised patience will be less annoyed by things that make him or her wait ('these stupid lifts', 'that slow cashier'). Someone who has developed an attitude of care for the environment will look differently at travel destinations and transport from someone who has not. A self-conscious person will interpret a silly remark differently from someone who constantly doubts him- or herself.

Someone wild and continuously seeking thrills will see an erotic adventure in what is an innocent flirtation to another.

Whatever we think we know about what is 'good' or what 'should be done' is not meaningless before we do it, but already determines the outcome. Our knowledge informs our perceptions and slowly shapes our attitude, and through that our actions as well. This long and gradual process is another characteristic of virtue ethics. It is not so much aiming for the solution of problems at hand, but it works in a 'precautionary' mode. Therefore, virtue ethics fits with hermeneutics as ethical method (Chapter II.2): the interpretation of moral experience proved to be oriented towards self-knowledge that would dispose us to act well. Virtue ethics does not prescribe what we should do or judge what we have done, but rather aims to form an attitude that makes us more suitable to act 'naturally' well. What training is for the athlete, what exercise is for the artist, what study is for the scientist, virtue or character education is for someone who tries to be as good as possible as a human being.

That is another reason why I choose virtue ethics over other ethical theories. I started this book by pointing out that ethics is not about living in the sense of survival, but about the art of living well in such a way that life has quality, that it is good, worthwhile, 'beautiful' as a work of art. In ethics we call this 'perfectionism'. Virtue ethics is a perfectionist ethic. It is not so much about the decent as about the excellent. 'Virtue' is the translation of the Latin word *virtus*, which means 'power', from which our word 'virtuosity' is derived. The Latin *virtus* itself was the translation of the Greek word *arete*, which refers to excellence: being very good at something.

This perfectionism should not be misunderstood. It does not mean that someone is only virtuous when he or she is perfect, or even worse: that everyone who is not perfect is not virtuous. That would be making perfection a standard everyone should meet. However, virtue is not a norm. Virtue is a strength that needs practice to become even stronger. So, virtue does not exist so much in full perfection, but in the focus on further perfection, in the interest in improvement and in the actual willingness to practise in order to improve. A scientist is no longer a (good) scientist as soon a he or she stops trying to become a better scientist. Friends are more virtuous as friends to the extent that they are focused on perfecting their friendship; lovers or partners are more virtuous as partners the more they are focused on not only keeping their love alive, but making it stronger, more intense, purer, more celebratory, in short: more beautiful.

This has also shown that perfectionism does not make virtue ethics into an overconfident, but rather a *modest,* form of ethics. It acknowledges that there is always room for improvement. The attention to perfection is also the recognition of the imperfection of what has been realized. This in no way implies a condemnation of the existing situation, provided that there exists a focus on improvement, as in the case of the athlete, the artist, the scientist and so on. In this sense, virtue ethics is a dynamic ethics. It is in line with people's ambition to grow, that is: to become stronger, braver, wiser, more moderate, fairer, in short: better.

The modesty of virtue ethics also lies in another important aspect, namely in the role of examples. Those who try to get better are mirroring those who can already do it better. My father loved working on the house in his spare time. Over a period of many years, he undertook work on room after room and gradually rebuilt the whole house. For me those were the days: those Saturdays and holiday weeks when he was working with his extensive collection of tools inherited for the most part from his father; despite the fact that, unlike my brothers and some of my sisters, I was not allowed to help. I had the reputation of being so clumsy that I did everything wrong and dropped everything, thus destroying more than contributing to any recovery. I was therefore condemned to watch; I did so for many hours and days: watching from a safe distance how my father used the tools and processed the materials. Much later, when I bought a house in which things had to be refurbished and decided to try it myself, it turned out that I was not so clumsy after all. Although I didn't have much practical experience yet, I had seen my father hold the chisel, use the plumbing, look when he sawed, and so on. It turned out that it was natural for me, to adopt the right attitude in all these activities because the image of how my father did it was engraved in my memory as an example. And anyone who has learned to saw in a straight line, or not to warp a nail, knows that the secret to success lies mainly in the posture.

The wisdom of the master–apprentice relationship lies in this: you only learn by first looking at the example and following it. This applies to manual labour, as well as to other activities. The famous Dutch writer Gerard Reve once said that anyone who wants to develop and improve his or her own style of writing should start by imitating their ideal writer as well as possible: to follow their example. The same applies to the domain of morality. If you want to try to act well, you have to look at how exemplary people do it.

Everyone has people around him or her whom he or she admires. Your father or mother or another family member, someone in your neighbourhood, a colleague, a teacher or someone you know from stories, from what you have seen of him or her or read in documentaries or biographies or autobiographies. People you admire, exemplary people, show you in a very concrete way what good actions are, and they make you realize that you already know this in a certain sense: after all, you already recognize it in the exemplary figures. By mirroring you learn to do it yourself. Moreover, it allows you to practise the most important of virtues: *prudence* (*phronèsis*, *prudentia*). This most hermeneutic of virtues consists, in fact, mainly in the ability to translate the ideal into actual situations or vice versa: to interpret the specific circumstances in terms of the moral ideal.

The role of example, therefore, implies a certain modesty, insofar as the example implies the acknowledgement that some are better than you. This can be extended to another interesting feature of the (Aristotelian) virtue ethics. Virtue ethics is more aware than any other ethics that people also differ morally, or even in terms of their talent. Just as there are not only better and lesser athletes, artists and scientists, and just as people are more or less suitable for running or playing the violin or arithmetic, so too do people differ morally and in talent. Of course, this does not alter the fact that minimum requirements can be imposed on everyone – but virtue ethics is not concerned with this. In this respect too, other forms of ethics are much more egalitarian than virtue ethics. It is not without reason that most other forms stem from modernity, in which the fundamental equality of all people has come to play such an important role. In Kantian ethics, the demand for equality has become the core of ethics; in utilitarianism, all interests count equally in the end; contractualism realizes equality through justice-creating procedures. Therefore, all these ethical theories make equal demands on everyone and ultimately bind everyone to the same standard in order to determine whether or not they live up to it.

Premodern virtue ethics can more easily do justice to what we all know than modern ethics: that moral quality also exists in gradations; some lives are better than others, more successful or happier. And for happiness you also need to have a certain talent, a talent not equally distributed among people. Those with a depressive disposition will not easily become happy, certainly not in a stable way. Every talent can of course be developed, but not by everyone to the same extent. You can cherish your predisposition to gloom, protect yourself by self-reproach against the expected reproaches of others and, by paying excessive attention to everything that may go wrong, try to arm yourself against the blows of fate. Some people look so much at everything that has failed in their lives that it seems as if that is the only way for them to hold on to their ideal without actually working on its (partial and gradual) realization. That way, one does not get any better. Only actual practice of the right kind can help, even if it may be difficult, painful or threatening for such people. But however important this exercise may be, it is possible that, even after a long time of perseverance, it does not yet produce the cheerfulness that others naturally have.

Finally, virtue ethics is perhaps best suited to the *interpretative* and *pluralistic* character of the hermeneutic ethics we have outlined. Not only do virtues exist in plural, but there isn't even a list of all virtues. Not because it has not yet been drawn up, but because every time and situation demands its own virtues. In Athens at the time of Aristotle, there was a specific name for the optimal way to deal with money and property (*eleutheriotes*) and another for the best way to deal with a lot of money (*megaloprepeia*). During the Christian Middle Ages, virtues were formulated that had never been thought of before (obedience, chastity, humility); in our own time, integrity and assertiveness are becoming virtues, which are nowhere to be found in any previous list of virtues. Perhaps one could say that virtues themselves are moral interpretations of moments of action and of the passions addressed by them. Because these moments and their conditions change, other passions, or aspects of them, are also addressed: contemporary management appeals to our desire for power and control; the disconnection between sexuality and reproduction affects our desire for love; the global and continuous supply of news does something with our desire for knowledge; the way in which social media constantly keeps us connected influences our desire for recognition.

All these changing circumstances are inevitably shaping us, but this formation can also be a *deformation*. The speed at which we can travel, work and communicate today does something to our ability to wait: it makes us impatient. Virtue ethics focuses our attention on this inevitable formation; it makes us realize that we are in fact always being formed, and tries to indicate what would be the best way, or how we can obtain optimal attitudes. What does patience mean, and how can we learn it in an age of acceleration? What is the difference between interest and curiosity and how can we shape our desire for information without becoming addicted to news? What does love and care mean for your children, and how can we learn this, in an age in which both parents have a job and crèches exist? How do you realize the choice for and loyalty to a partner at a time when serial monogamy seems to have become the most common form of relationship?

Desires sometimes seem opposite: you want to be responsible *and* to enjoy; you want to be loyal *and* follow your heart, you want to plan ahead but *also* be open to the unexpected. However, the tension may lie in the fact that the different desires are badly formed or not formed at all. Well-formed desires do not often contradict each other. Responsibility and pleasure can find each other in a measured attitude: measured enjoyment is not less enjoyment, but better enjoyment. Loyalty and passion may find each other in openness and honesty. A passion that is expressed is less compelling, and loyalty that is open-hearted does not become a prison. Looking ahead cautiously does not have to define the future or exclude all risks, but can also consist of an open attitude full of expectations.

Virtues are moral interpretations of action situations and passions, in the sense that they represent those attitudes that give the relevant passions the best possible shape in the given circumstances. They indicate what a person looks like who, in relation to these kinds of situations, flourishes, succeeds, is happy and turns his or her life into something good, beautiful and worthwhile.

2 The art of living well

One of the most popular schools of philosophy today is the so-called philosophy of the art of living well. This movement itself is too extensive to summarize in brief – especially if one takes the history of the art of living well as broadly as some authors do. Michel Foucault, for example, was one of the founders of this school through his studies of the ancient philosophies; these involved a cultivation of the 'care for oneself', a core concept in the philosophy of Plato. Foucault was inspired by Pierre Hadot, a historian of philosophy, who developed his thesis on 'philosophy as a way of life' mainly on the basis of studies of Hellenistic philosophy. In Germany, his books on the art of living well made Wilhelm Schmid a best-selling author. His success began with a book about Michel Foucault and his significance for ethics. This was followed by a study in which many authors from the history of philosophy were placed within the framework of the art of living well. In the Netherlands the work of Joep Dohmen is no less popular. In the first of his ever-expanding series of books on the art of living well (2007), he presented an anthology of texts by great thinkers from the past who, according to him, had all written about the art of living well; in one of his most recent books (2010; at least, his most recent as I write this), he collects a large part of contemporary practical philosophy on the denominator of the art of living well. With this, the art of living well does what every school of philosophy seems to do (and what I also did in the previous chapter with regard to hermeneutic ethics): reread history in the light of its own design. Such a rereading is always interesting: it connects new steps with history and makes the new sound a voice in the ongoing conversation of tradition. However, it should not erase the differences between the various voices.

While Joep Dohmen (2010: 100) presents Aristotelian virtue ethics as 'a variation of the art of living well', I will focus in this chapter on a difference between these two traditions. And in my concise and selective presentation of the art of living well I will try to show different kinds of it, by a representation of the thoughts of Pierre Hadot on the one hand and a short characterization of recent work by Dohmen and Schmid on the other. Incidentally, we will see that both types of 'the art of living well', despite their differences, have an important common trait; one that I will contrast with an element from the tradition of virtue ethics.

2.1 Pierre Hadot: philosophy as a way of life

Pierre Hadot (1922–2010) was (just like his wife Ilsetraut) an expert in Hellenistic philosophy, within which he gave Stoicism a special position. His work in the field of history of philosophy, however, pretends to say something about what philosophy essentially is: first and foremost a way of life. This is the most important characteristic in which 'the art of living well' as it appears in Hadot's work distinguishes itself from the way in which later authors, who refer to him, use that term: it is not so much about the way in which philosophy can be an instrument or advisor to make life a work of art, but that the good life essentially consists of nothing but philosophizing. To this end, he shows, on the basis of historical studies, what philosophy actually is. In the following I will rely on several of Hadot's books about ancient philosophy, especially his *What is Ancient Philosophy?* (2004) and *Philosophy as a Way of Life* (1995).

According to Hadot, philosophy is – from its first beginning, early in the sixth century BC, at the edge of the Greek world – first and foremost a way of life, and one that is characterized by an existential choice for a 'life of the mind', accompanied by an explanation and justification of this way of living, and which is cultivated by a system of 'spiritual exercises'. These exercises aim to help in bringing about what is important in such a life, that is: a radical transformation of the self. The fact that today we see philosophy rather as a theory that has nothing to do with the author's way of living, is the result of a development that according to Hadot started in the Middle Ages, and to which I will come back briefly later.

According to Hadot, philosophy is, in its original, spiritual meaning, indeed theory, but it is not an isolated theory; it is part of a chosen way of life. This does not make theoretical reflection less important: a life without theoretical guidance and justifications runs the risk of becoming banal, colourless or sentimental; but a theory without the corresponding way of life does not lead to philosophy, but only sophistry. The theory provides a critical test for the chosen way of life and prevents certain practices from acquiring a meaning they do not deserve. It also strengthens the choice made by justifying it and shielding it from arbitrariness. The theory also serves the way of life in another way: philosophical thinking requires peace, concentration and self-examination. Those who fly restlessly from one to the other cannot think well; since philosophy is a form of non-empirical-scientific and hardly paradigmatic theorizing, it has little other protection against self-deception than a continuous critical self-examination. The philosopher will have to be willing and able to be alone, in critical conversation with his own thoughts. Well, these characteristics of philosophy are also characteristics of the life chosen, and philosophy thus helps to give the chosen life the required peace, concentration, loneliness and self-criticism.

This already shows that, in the art of living well as conceived by Hadot, theory is not so much a means in the service of the chosen way of life; it is, itself an essential part of this way of life. The chosen life is a life of the mind; contemplation is an essential part of it. This means that we should see theory, or *theorein* in Greek, also as praxis – even as the highest performance of the praxis of life. Wisdom itself is a skill; the theory itself is the best praxis and the cultivated philosophical life is the highest form of happiness, the successful life, the art of living well. However much the differences between the different theories may be of importance for the way in which the chosen way of life is critically tested, those differences are put into perspective at the same time, as far as all theories concern the praxis of philosophical life itself.

This should not be understood as if one could ever be done with that way of living. We should rather say that its completion is ever further away and that wisdom is an ideal that can only be approached asymptotically, that is to say: without ever fully coinciding with that ideal. It is a well-known topos of Hellenistic philosophy in particular, that there have been no or hardly any real 'sages'. Socrates may be the only generally accepted exception, but for itself Socrates was more of a person who was constantly searching than resting in his wisdom. The wisdom he claimed consisted precisely in realizing not to know and thus – to seek. The philosophical life can therefore rather be considered as a spiritual process of searching and therefore of transformation that has become a second nature. It also points to something it can never take possession of, and perhaps not even put into words. It is a life that is an ongoing exercise in wisdom, meaning that it consists in forming and transforming. Philosophy is a continuous exercise in a way of life, and transforming that way of life.

Because according to Hadot philosophy is first and foremost a way of life, everything it consists of must be seen as an instrument for that life, as an exercise to realize it, or as a cultivation of that way of life. All these exercises, which by the way can be very physical, are in the service of 'a life of the mind', and can therefore be called 'spiritual exercises'. Let us look more closely at what these exercises consist of and what they aim to realize.

Plato made mathematics (geometry) a compulsory prerequisite for entering his academy and in the education in Plato's state one has to study arithmetic, geometry, stereometry, astronomy and harmony for ten years before starting philosophy (*Politeia*, Book VII). The main reason for this is not so much the knowledge that a student of philosophy should have, but the way of life that the practice of science entails and the way of thinking with which someone should be familiar or in which he or she should be proficient. The sciences 'serve to protect the mind from emotional imaginations'. Generally speaking, the sciences are an exercise in concentration and pure thought; in this sense, the practice of science is a spiritual exercise.

For most of the philosophers of the Hellenistic schools, philosophy consisted of ethics, logics and (meta)physics. Both logic and physics were mostly subordinate to ethics, which explicitly dealt with living in the right way. The Stoics, for instance, taught logics in order to be able to judge correctly, so that one avoids, in a correct judgement, feelings or emotions that without sufficient reason attribute a certain significance to the event under consideration. Those who judge correctly will not allow their judgement that, for example, a river might flood very soon, to be clouded by feelings of anxiety. Physics is a theory about nature that shows how it is controlled by *logos*. Anyone who learns to see the order of nature through knowledge of it will be able to make an easier assessment of that great nature when considering what is happening in their own lives. He or she can 'look at himself from above'. Hadot therefore also speaks of 'physics as spiritual exercise'.

Each school had its own method of teaching philosophy. But apart from the elements they have in common, the things that are different are all at the service of the exercise in the chosen life. Plato's dialogues are not written to inform, but to transform; they are an example of the dialectic of an exercise in self-examination which encourages it; not a purely logical exercise, but rather a spiritual exercise which requires of the interlocutors an asceticism, a transformation of themselves. Texts such as the *Encheiridion* (*The Handbook*) of Epictetus are distinctive for another method of education: it is mainly about learning to memorize the most important rules of life, so that they will be available at all times. The strict deduction-argumentative form of more systematic treatises is also intended to facilitate remembrance. Sceptical arguments act as purgative or purification, and the stories of the cynics, whose teaching (like that of Zen masters) sometimes does not exist in words but in a confrontational behaviour, show yet another way in which students can be trained in the chosen way of life. And even if the philosophical argument becomes scholastic and largely consists of explaining and commenting on important texts, this can first and foremost be seen as a spiritual exercise: an exercise in modesty, for example, that submits to the text.

In all the different schools, the teacher plays a central role. The teacher is a spiritual guide, who guides the student. That is why in many texts the living voice of the teacher can still be heard, not only in the Platonic dialogues, but also in the texts of Aristotle based on lectures, the conversations of Epictetus and the letters of Epicurus and Seneca. Ilsetraut Hadot, especially, has written extensively about the philosopher as spiritual director.

We have already established that ancient philosophy is mostly organized in schools. Sometimes (as with Plato) these schools may have had a political purpose, but they were mainly focused on the realization of the philosophical life itself. Most schools were more than just places of instruction. The teacher and the (core group of) pupils lived together there. The meals, at least, were enjoyed together and ideally a bond of friendship connected the members of a school. Daily and confidential contact between pupils and teachers was important for the exercise in the chosen way of life. This friendship is a kind of sublimated love that 'is the privileged means to achieve the transformation of self', because one can only learn from those one loves. The love for the teacher makes the student obey blindly before he or she is able to understand the justification of the teacher's authority. The mutual help and correction among the students, as well as and especially the teaching and spiritual guidance by the teacher were thus supported by an affective bond.

The communal life in the school, this practice of public confession of one's faults; mutual correction, carried out in a fraternal spirit; examining one's conscience, was very conducive to what was perhaps the most important thing for those who had chosen the life of the spirit. The practice of continuous self-examination, which the tradition of Christian spirituality had called the examination of conscience, is central to all schools. Self-knowledge requires living together with friends who act as mirrors in which one can observe oneself. Pupils are trained to examine their day both in the evening before going to bed and in the morning when they wake up to determine what they consider their task for the day. Examining one's own dreams helps to discover hidden desires. The different methods of self-examination allow the learner to distinguish between the one he or she is actually, the one who judges him- or herself and the one who he or she aspires to be – an important distinction for those who have embarked on the path of transformation!

Much of the work on this transformation consists of being freed from what keeps us from it. Thus, by learning to judge correctly and acquiring true knowledge about nature, one can free oneself from unreal desires. By means of a regular *praemeditatio malorum* (an anticipatory reflection on possible evil that may affect you), among which the *praemeditatio mortis* (a reflection on one's own mortality) occupies an important place, one can discover that what is dreaded as an evil is not an evil, but an aspect of reality as a whole, which is well constructed. This **praemeditatio** with which you *prepare for a future* is paradoxically also an exercise to *live in the present*: whoever realizes that what happens to us does not depend on ourselves, can free him- or herself from anxious worries and enjoy the moment. By practising moderation and abstaining from sensory pleasures, one can free oneself from addiction to a way of life that is guided by the body rather than the mind. Keeping the body healthy prevents it from becoming an obstacle to spiritual growth and hardening it makes one less susceptible to suffering. The latter underlines once again that the body was also involved in the 'spiritual exercises' of philosophy. In some schools, breathing exercises were a recurring element of the programme. From the beginning of Greek education or *paideia*, it was aimed at the whole person and therefore consisted of a combination of medicine, sport and spiritual direction.

All these exercises – in Hellenistic philosophy as interpreted by Hadot – are aimed at a life that is called 'spiritual'; not because it is no longer the life of physically living people, but because in that life the body no longer determines what I should do but the mind, or I myself. The exercises are focused on the life in which I take the lead, or better: on the transformation of the person that is needed for that.

Many of the exercises are about liberation from what threatens to hold us back: our passions and desires, our bodies, sensory impressions and the world of sensory things. Asceticism is aimed at preventing the body from attracting attention; it thus frees attention for the mind and thus helps 'to bring about a change in self'. These exercises are certainly not about denying the body or the world or making ourselves blind or insensitive to it. However, they help us to make sure that we let nothing else but true knowledge of the world and the body determine our judgement about what is happening in the world (some disaster for example) or about what we perceive about our body (some passionate love for example). And by purifying our judgement in this way we can prevent ourselves from becoming the prisoners of our own passions and senses or of the events in the world. For this we will also have to detach ourselves from the mass, which is controlled by irrational desires and emotions.

The spiritual exercises are thus aimed at acquiring freedom in the sense of autarchy and peace of mind. The differences between schools during the Hellenistic period are largely the result of the fact that they identify the threat to peace of mind in different ways: for one it is pleasure, for another it is false pleasure, for another it is false judgement, for another it is fear (especially fear of death). The remedy is always sought in a kind of indifference for what does not matter. First and foremost, this requires that we know how to distinguish between what does and does not depend on us. Without the training that philosophy offers, we would remain at the mercy of all kinds of forces and powers, with all the restlessness and uncertainty that this entails.

By the way, the forces that keep us imprisoned for the most part lie in ourselves, in our own desire, our own pretensions and so on. That is why a large part of the exercise will be aimed at mastering that 'actual' self. This 'self-control' can for example also be achieved by ascetic practices; the exercise in abstinence is only aimed at one's own self regaining control over one's own desires. The humility with which a student has to submit to the teacher, or in later time to the authoritative text, is also such an exercise, aimed at freeing oneself from subjective pretensions.

In addition to freeing ourselves from what holds us captive, these spiritual exercises of philosophy teach us to see reality as dominated and governed by reason. Understanding the reasonableness of the world order makes it possible for it no longer to clash with our desires, to the extent that we have also learned to control our own desires through our reasonableness. In this way what is especially known as the great ideal of Stoic ethics becomes possible: the consent to nature. In the other schools we find a similar ideal in one form or another. In all of them it is a life somehow dedicated to the *theoria*.

Aristotle calls this a divine life and says that it is not attainable for humankind in a sustainable way. And this idea too we find in different ways throughout the (Ancient) tradition. The sage is an ideal rather than a real possibility. If there has ever been a wise man, then – as has been said – it might be Socrates, who has become mythical. Epicurus too seems to have been regarded by his pupils as the incorporation of that wisdom. However, according to most thinkers and schools there never was a wise man. Hadot writes: 'In this transcendent norm established by reason, each school will express its own vision of the world, its own style of life, and its idea of the perfect man' (Hadot 1995).

The two sides of the spiritual exercises I mentioned can be summarized and put together as follows: the victory over one's own pride and the knowledge of the greater whole in which one stands, for someone who gets to know this great order discovers at the same time his own true greatness, namely in the ability to comprehend the whole of things. But for this to happen, the self that has wrongly identified itself with the whole, or at least as the centre of the whole, must be eliminated. In other words: only when one no longer sees everything from the limited perspective of one's own self can one elevate oneself to a universal perspective. Without the asceticism of moderation and humility, the self stands in the way of its own true greatness.

The reader may think that all this sounds rather religious and even Christian. Hadot may have been a priest for a period of time, but he would certainly reject the association between his thesis and Christianity on several key points. But before I go into that in more detail (see the end of this chapter), I will now focus on a few other representatives of the contemporary art of living well.

2.2 Wilhelm Schmid and Joep Dohmen: the art of living well as self-responsibility

In a benevolent interpretation of the contemporary philosophy of the art of living well, one could say that it attempts to make philosophy what it should be according to Hadot and actually was in antiquity: a practice serving the good life. Still a crucial difference is the fact that according to Hadot the good life is a philosophical life, while philosophy in the contemporary art of living well is at most instrumental for the good life. Because the contemporary philosophy of the art of living well does not primarily describe what philosophy was in Hellenism, but rather tries to give people today instructions for a 'beautiful' or 'happy' life, very different elements or nuances emerge in those indications than in the work of Hadot.

In this section I do not want to elaborate on the differences and similarities between the recent philosophy of the art of living well and Hadot's 'philosophy as a way of life', but I will try to sketch this contemporary philosophy on the basis of some recent publications by German philosopher Wilhelm Schmid and Dutch philosopher Joep Dohmen. I do not pretend to give a complete summary of their work, but will try to find out what they think 'the art of living well' actually is, and then focus on a few characteristics of their understanding of this philosophy. This implies that I only pay attention to the similarities in their work and that I do not address the (in my opinion, minor) differences between them.

The contemporary philosophy of the art of living well tends to present itself as an adaptation of ancient ethics, and in particular virtue ethics, to the circumstances of post-, late- or otherwise modern people. These are people who live in what the German sociologist Ulrich Beck has called a 'risk society': a world of uncertainty and insecurity, in which people no longer have a foothold in tradition and convention or social structures, in which they are inevitably primarily individuals and in this sense individualists, and in which they, in their search for how to live, realize that there is no destiny of life in nature.

Some of these conditions (in particular the uncertainty and the absence of a footing in tradition and social structure) also apply to the

Hellenistic period, the period of the great empires of Alexander the Great, of his successors and later the Roman field lords, consuls and emperors. Even then, people were confused by the incomprehensibility of the world in which they lived, by the many cultures that had been gathered within an empire, by the plethora of philosophies that presented themselves, and by the daily hectic. It is, therefore, no coincidence that the philosophical schools from that period seem to be a strong source of inspiration for the current art of living well. The other conditions are typically modern and different from what was self-evident in antiquity. For us, nature is no longer a predetermined order to which we must conform, but material that we must learn to control: humans are not primarily social beings, but the community is secondary and composed of individuals.

Late Ancient as well as modern conditions apparently determine the constellation in which contemporary humans live. These mixed influences may also be the reason why our present historical period does not really have its own name (such as antiquity, the Middle Ages, Modernity, or such as Hellenism, scholasticism, Renaissance, romanticism), but is only called 'post-', or 'late-' or 'otherwise modern'. Nietzsche writes that our identity lies in not having our own identity but being the collection of everything that has been there. In the art of living well, we do indeed see a mix of elements from ancient and modern theories, albeit in such a way that all these elements change through their merging.

Aristotelian virtue ethics is undoubtedly an important background for the art of living well. In both cases (virtue ethics and the art of living well) it is about an ethic of self-realization, i.e. the development of the self as best as possible. This ideal of self-realization is also expressed in the art of living well as 'an ideal of personal excellence' and as virtuosity, or better: as excellent attitudes. Both in the art of living well and in virtue ethics, action takes place in practices (more or less standardized and patterns of action that are recognizable within a community), and the used concept of action is that of *praxis* and not of *poiesis*: 'The purpose of life does not lie [...] in the end product. The path itself is the goal', as Joep Dohmen writes. And the way in which the goal is achieved is no different than the way in which according to Aristotle virtue is created, that is by 'practising, practising, practising', or by forming good habits. As in the tradition of virtue ethics, Schmid considers the so-called cardinal virtues as the most important ones: reason, justice, courage and measure frequently appear in his work. Here again, measure is not fundamentally the most important, but in fact the most widely used virtue; here too, it seems to exist in a kind of middle: 'a viable measure between a surplus and a deficit' (Schmid 2004: 29), a middle that is differentiated in the same way as for Aristotle (in which situation, with regard to whom, how long, to what extent, etc.).

In addition to these similarities, however, there are also remarkable differences, among other things because Hellenistic (especially stoic) and modern elements are also introduced into the art of living well. In this way, elements slip into the art of living well that quite sharply differ from each of the earlier positions, on a number of points. I will try to name the most important of these elements.

Joep Dohmen writes the following 'The ethics of the art of living well [. . .] is based on an authentic, personal search for what is of value to you. Self-development is in the service of realizing that value orientation and being faithful to yourself in it' (Dohmen 2010: 174). Wilhelm Schmid seems to distinguish his philosophy of the art of living well from an ethic, or at least from 'morality', because of this purpose of the art of living well: (one's own) freedom. He presents his rules for life 'not primarily for moral reasons, but for the sake of preserving that freedom' (Schmid 2004: 152). Morality seems to be identified with a restriction of freedom that is necessary for the equal freedom of all others. In the art of living well, on the other hand, the main concern would not be the equal freedom of others, but the cultivation of one's own freedom. If the art of living well were to be an 'ethic', it would be an 'aesthetic ethic', that is: an ethic that transcends 'a moral context'.

This ethic (I keep using this word) is about self-care, about the cultivation of one's own individual freedom and of responsibility for one's own life. Of course, this also includes how one should relate to others. One of the books by Wilhelm Schmid is, according to the subtitle, 'about the art of living well in dealing with others'. However, this interaction with others is within the framework and in the spirit of the project that aims to turn one's own life into a work of art. According to Schmid, justice is 'a basic condition for a beautiful life'; however, even justice is 'first and foremost a problem of self in dealing with oneself' (Schmid 2004: 125). Caring for others remains a question of whether it fits into one's own life plan, and is only important when and to what extent one 'considers it appropriate' (Dohmen 2007: 193). Dohmen does speak of a 'new collective morality', but the only collective thing here is that one inevitably practises self-care in the presence of others. Real responsibility for others, let alone the possibility that your own life project will be disturbed by the appeal of others: that is not really possible in this framework. At most it might be added to the art of living well through its connection with the ethics of care. Dohmen even criticizes philosophers who, as he suggests, instrumentalize self-care, and didn't really care much about self-care, freedom and autonomy, but more about solidarity – apparently that is not what the art of living well is about.

It seems that there are no values – social or otherwise – that have been given and to which we must adhere. On the contrary: the moral task consists primarily in finding, inventing and creating your own moral orientation, partly by means of self-knowledge, and in realizing this through practice. 'Authentic self-care' consists of 'attempting to be the editor of one's own life story' (Dohmen 2007: 189), taking control of oneself or one's own life (Schmid 2001: 7). This can be done by acquiring self-knowledge, practising the ability to act, finding your own values and learning to deal with your situatedness, especially: your temporality and the social conditions in which you live. It is important to learn who you are, what you want and how you can accomplish this, so you can 'coincide' with yourself, can 'appropriate' yourself (Dohmen 2010: 188).

Sometimes it seems as if intellectualism has returned from antiquity. According to Socrates, moral quality can ultimately be reduced to true knowledge of the good. In Stoicism, this reappears in a modified form, when it states that virtue consists primarily in correct judgement and then considers it to be a sufficient condition for happiness. In philosophy of the art of living well, true knowledge of the good is replaced by authentic knowledge of and choice for one's own self. However, the scheme is similar: in the end you have your own happiness in your hands, as long as you know yourself and act authentically. It is true that you must try to be 'good where and when it really matters', but what it means, 'to be good', and when it 'matters', you ultimately choose that yourself.

The values to which we commit and that determine what we want are themselves the objects of our own choice. Schmid always emphasizes that his 'art of living' only presents options without prescribing a certain norm. However evaluating and even judgemental his texts may be, he himself writes that even a recommendation would still be too prescriptive. Not only do you have to learn to discover and understand, yourself, which values are guiding your life, but you also have to decide for yourself in every situation which action from which value is appropriate. Everything becomes a matter of choice, even the way you choose and the criterion on the basis of which you choose. 'The art of living, whatever its content may look like, is entirely based on the choice made by the subject' (Schmid 2001: 26). Of course these philosophers acknowledge that one does not do this alone, but together with others; but one also chooses who are the 'meaningful others' for one (Dohmen 2010: 62, 89). This can be done, for example, by experimenting; in other words, by 'trying out' who is or is not meaningful to you. You also decide for yourself whether or not you should be loyal.

'Self-responsibility' is, therefore, an important concept in this ethics of the art of living well. It consists of the attempt to control and steer the course of your life to a certain extent, by taking a greater role in the direction and the quality of your life based on your own understanding and the capacity to act accordingly (Dohmen 2007: 37). Of course Dohmen too is well aware that we can only control that life 'to a certain extent', and that people remain 'vulnerable and dependent beings', but that vulnerability always only appears in the margin of his text. The text itself is about 'controlling on the basis of good self-management' (2007: 39).

Therefore, I have to rectify what I wrote earlier: there does appear to be a value given in advance, namely *authenticity*; according to Dohmen the bottom line of the art of living living well. Faithfulness to the other may be something you can choose for or against, but one has to be faithful to oneself in an absolute sense. As with all absolute values, it does not appear that authenticity can be further justified or founded. Authenticity is 'simply a must', and the art of living well consists in acquiring it.

There is also no doubt for these authors that this 'art to master life' is a difficult task, but in the end it is possible for whoever wants it. Choosing, for example, is difficult and painful, but describing the difficulty makes it clear that there is a solution: 'The obstacles [...] are numerous: lack of discipline, time and concentration, pain of uncertainty, possible mistakes, repression – all this can keep us from self-examination' (Dohmen 2010: 134). Indeed, if these are the problems, then they are, however difficult, solvable: 'To choose you have to make a hierarchy of desires and reject certain desires. Which desires are really important to you, which desires do you want to satisfy, which are given priority, which fit you as a person? You must get to know yourself and determine your structure of desires and volitions' (Dohmen 2010: 121 in reference to the works of Peter Bieri). Success ultimately depends on your own commitment and effort. Of course these thinkers too know that it is not always easy and that your own will can prevent you 'as it were from somewhere outside of you', but again, there is a solution for that: 'You can solve this by trying to better understand this will'. You are solely responsible. The philosophy of art of living well is about 'a specific morality of self-responsibility' (Dohmen 2010: 113).

3 The art of living well, virtue ethics and the human deficit

The example of the will, one's own will, which nevertheless presents itself as a stranger, reminds us of the great inner conflict that Augustine describes in the eighth book of his *Confessions*, written in the fourth century AD. He wants to be converted, but at the same time he does not want it and resists against it. It is as if he does not coincide with his own will, or better: as if he does not want to coincide with himself. His own will turns out to be divided, split – and so he feels powerless but responsible at the same time.

In a way, even in an eminent one, Augustine then did what the philosophers of the art of living well recommended: he began to try to 'better understand his will'. Augustine thereby became – as we will see in the next chapter (IV.3.2) – the one who discovered the will in the true sense. Greek philosophy did not really know the faculty that we now call the will. So it is thanks to Augustine that we can now speak about the will as the philosophy of the art of living well does. However, he discovered that faculty as something paradoxical: the faculty which make that I am in charge and can choose autonomously, precisely that faculty appears to be so divided that it makes me powerless. At the heart of their power, according to Augustine, humans are powerless.

I think that the philosophy of the art of living well pays too little attention to this powerlessness, our impotence, our weakness, our vulnerability. When there is vulnerability in Dohmen's concept of the art of living well, it is almost always the vulnerability of others. One's own vulnerability is only recognized dutifully; often at the end of a chapter, very briefly and to be immediately followed by a plea for the resilience we need to develop against it. The 'tragic human condition' seems to disappear into our own 'self-responsibility' – just as in the intellectualist positions of antiquity; with the difference that the ancient 'true knowledge of the good' has now been replaced by 'knowledge of and choice for the authentic self'. Contemporary philosophers of the art of living well do state that there is no perfect strategy, but what they set against it, the discovery of one's own limits, immediately includes the task of relating oneself to these limits. And with that they at least suggest that we also can and should take back into our own hands that which we do not control.

By this failure to recognize or by underestimating our powerlessness and vulnerability, the art of living well also pays little attention to the extent to which human life is inevitably suffering. Schmid does acknowledge that – for example with regard to love – life is a great deal of suffering, but his book suggests that this suffering can largely, if not completely, be removed by his philosophy of living well. We only have to learn to moderate our desire, to realize that there is a difference between possibility and reality, and to accept that difference. He even calls it an *ontological* diffierence and defines the art of living well as 'the conscious effort to befriend the ontological difference between reality and possibility and to learn to move along in the interaction between the two' (2010: 115). What is split in the experience of love (longing and saturation, attracting and repelling, eternity and temporariness), is reconciled – or put aside – by him by speaking of the 'wave principle' of love or of the 'breathing love'. The remaining suffering is simply a part of love and is robbed of its repulsive nature by the fact that even that becomes a matter of one's own choice: 'The individual must choose which kind of suffering he wants to prefer' (Schmid 2010: 84).

The philosophy of the art of living well shares this emphasis on self-activation and growth through practice with virtue ethics, but the naive and optimistic belief in its success is certainly not found in the latter. Admittedly, virtue ethics is also an ethics of self-realization and self-improvement. Nevertheless, it is aware of and does justice to human vulnerability and powerlessness. I briefly recall the ways in which virtue ethics shows a modesty that seems to be alien to the described art of living well.

'Happiness' or 'flourishing' and 'virtue' are the two key concepts of virtue ethics. The first I discussed in Chapter II (II.3), and we saw that happiness is a concept that contains a certain tension and that, because of that, it can never be fully realized. While virtue ethics tries to show what you should do and how you should live in order to succeed or to flourish and become happy, it – or at least Aristotle, the father of virtue ethics – at the same time acknowledges that we do not totally control happiness ourselves: one also needs a bit of luck. Earlier in this chapter (III.1) we saw that the concept of virtue implies modesty in several ways and, moreover, is linked to the recognition that people are also different and have different talents in terms of their moral competences. To be virtuous, one does not only need one's own talents, but also the help of others and circumstances. Martha Nussbaum, one of the authors who contributed to the regained popularity of virtue ethics, published a book on the fragility of happiness, but also of goodness (1986). On the basis of Greek tragedies, she shows moral conflicts make it that sometimes evil is inevitable: Agamemnon can only assume his political and military responsibility by going against his duties towards his family. In other ways, too, the moral quality of our actions and the happiness they bring us is not entirely in our power: moral quality requires trust in people and in the world – and trust can be seriously harmed. The story of Hecuba, once Queen of Troy, shows how even the possibility of a dignified human life can be taken away from moral people, through no fault of their own.

Both the reduction of happiness to virtue and that of virtue to what is in our own hands, we also find in the philosophy of the art of living well, so that it contains more of Stoic wisdom than of Aristotelian virtue. However, this Stoic wisdom is often all too 'clever' (read, for example, Seneca's letters to Lucilius) and much less lifelike than the art of living well claims to be. In a way, the art of living well magnifies this unrealistic character of stoicism. At least most Stoics acknowledged the fact that their ideal of life was so difficult to realize, that it had never actually been done by anyone – except, perhaps, by Socrates. By the way, this acknowledgement turns into a grotesque farce when one starts imitating Socrates – as Seneca did when he staged his own death, following the story of Socrates as told in Plato's *Critio*. Seneca at least considered himself an exception, while the philosophy of the art of living well suggests that happiness is attainable to everyone, by just working hard.

The philosophy of the art of living well is a curious mix of elements of classical virtue ethics (with emphasis on exercise and self-improvement, aimed at a 'thriving', flourishing or happy life), the Hellenistic emphasis on one's own happiness (indifferent to what we do not control) and the modern belief in autonomy and one's own abilities. This seems to be a very short summary of a two-and-a-half-thousand-year-long tradition: from *c.*400 BC until now. This summary lacks the so-called 'Middle Ages'. The name 'Middle Ages' alone suggests how this period of history was neglected by the period in which the name was invented: Renaissance thinking looked back to antiquity, and early modern thinkers looked to the future. As a result, a very important element of European cultural history remains undetected, an element that has, however, left its mark on the development of virtue ethics – even if many contemporary publications on virtues often still neglect it.

Indeed, virtue ethics does not completely coincide with the ethics of Aristotle and its Hellenistic reception, but has developed during a long history of multiple innovations. Precisely in connection with the attention paid to the fragility of happiness and morality, and to the weakness and incapacity of humankind, a very important stage in this development is that in which Greek philosophy was incorporated by Christianity, and in which these two roots of European culture merged – also with regard to virtue ethics. I will elaborate on that development in the next chapter.

To conclude this chapter, I would just like to point out that it is precisely this phase in the history of virtue ethics that is remarkably *absent* from today's philosophy of the art of living well. Schmid shows that he does not know the so-called theological virtues (more about this in Chapter IV.3.3) when he includes Christian charity among the 'cooperative relations' defined by reciprocity (Schmid 2010: 62). Dohmen is somewhat indiscriminate and pitying about 'the Christian lifestyle'. It is, according to him, 'a form of self-development', but only in terms of 'humbly renouncing your own will and respecting the virtues of faith, hope and charity' (Dohmen 2010: 187). According to Dohmen, the Christian lifestyle is, therefore, an 'expropriated' one. Hadot, who himself had been a priest, and in whose 'philosophy as a way of life' many Christian elements are included, nevertheless (or therefore?) vehemently resisted the 'surnaturalism' with which Christianity would undermine its own responsibility.

For all three, the chorus is the same: Christianity does not do justice to our own responsibility. I suspect, on the other hand, that the philosophy of the art of living well inflates this own responsibility to such an extent that it does not do justice to real life. In the next chapter we will see how the Christian tradition can provide an important counterbalance in this respect.

Literature

Augustine (1961), *Confessions*, (translated by R.S. Pine-Coffin) London: Penguin.

Augustine (2004), *The City of God*, (translated by H. Bettenson, Penguin Classic) London: Penguin.

Dohmen, Joep (2007), *Tegen de onverschilligheid: Pleidooi voor een moderne levenskunst*, Amsterdam: Ambo.

Dohmen, Joep (2010), *Brief aan een middelmatige man: Pleidooi voor een nieuwe publieke moraal*, Amsterdam: Ambo.

Gadamer, H.-G. (1976), 'Hermeneutik als praktische Philosophie', in *Vernunft im Zeitalter der Wissenschaft*, 78–109, Frankfurt: Suhrkamp.

Hadot, Pierre (1995), *Philosophy as a Way of Life*, trans. M. Chase, Malden, MA/Oxford: Blackwell.

Hadot, Pierre (2004), *What is Ancient Philosophy?* Harvard University Press.

Nussbaum, Martha C. (1986), *The Fragility of Goodness: Luck and Ethics in Greek Tragedy and Philosophy*, Cambridge: Cambridge University Press.

Schmid, Wilhelm (1991), *Auf der Suche nach einer neuen Lebenskunst: Die Frage nach dem Grund und die Neubrgüündung der Ethik bei Foucault*, Frankfurt: Suhrkamp.

Schmid, Wilhelm (2010), *Die Liebe neu erfinden: Von der Lebenskunst im Umgang mit Anderen*, Frankfurt: Suhrkamp.

Tongeren, Paul van (2000), 'Virtues', in D. De Stexhe and J. Verstraeten (eds), *Matter of Breath: Foundations for Professional Ethics*, 227–38, Leuven: Peeters.

Tongeren, Paul van (2003), *Deugdelijk leven: Een inleiding in de deugdethiek*, Amsterdam: SUN/Boom.

Tongeren, Paul van (2008), 'Philosophy as a Form of Spirituality', in H. Blommestijn, C. Caspers, R. Hofman, F. Mertens, P. Nissen and H. Welzen (eds), *Seeing the Seeker: Explorations in the Discipline of Spirituality, Festschrift for Kees Waaijman*, 109–21, Leuven/Paris/Dudley: Peeters.

Love

In one of his *Letters to Educated Labourers* (Utrecht: Veen, 1985: 100) Dutch author Gerard Reve writes:

> I can give love to a reasonable degree, but it is very difficult to receive and accept love, apparently because I'm afraid of losing it again.

Everyone knows that love is not only beautiful, but very often difficult as well; however, we usually think the difficulty lies more in *giving* love – we all want to *be loved*, after all! Gerard Reve reminds us that being loved by someone else has its problems too. The reason he gives for this points to its risky nature: anything you simply get can be lost, it seems. We prefer to insure ourselves against all risks. And one way to do this is not to accept the thing you might lose.

In particular, when accepting love also implies your love for the other, you will become very dependent. After all, you cannot love someone solely on the condition that he or she loves you back. But is unconditional love possible? Yet it seems that you would have to love unconditionally to be able to love without fear, not to be afraid that your love will pass by. Is it because of this difficulty that lovers so often say 'I love you'? Are they perhaps doing that to ask the other person to say the same thing?

The insecurity that is attached to love also has to do with something else: at some point the loved one will wonder whether the lover actually loves who he or she really is. Doesn't he or she love his *image* of me, and doesn't that image deviate from who I really am? Does he or she know the other side of me? Would he or she still love me if he or she really knew me?

Gerard Reve's remark I quoted is about the relationship between faith and love. The complete passage reads as follows:

Faith and love are one, because faith is the ability to love unconditionally. And because my love is flawed in many ways, my faith is also flawed. I can give love to a reasonable degree, but it is very difficult to receive and accept love, apparently because I'm afraid of losing it again. My unbelief is the lack of sufficient courage to accept the Love of God.

If, against this background, we look again at that second cause of uncertainty in love, perhaps another reason appears for the difficulty of receiving or accepting love. The gift of love can be a curious kind of obligation, namely to be or to become the one you are in the eyes of the one who loves you, to accept that you are as he or she already knows you. Perhaps your authentic or true self is not what is hidden from the other, but something you yourself do not yet know. Perhaps the other person knows you better than you dare to know yourself: Love's knowledge.

The religious context is important, because it is God (who is called 'Love') who knows us better than we do ourselves. This is beautifully expressed in Psalm 139. It starts like this:

O Lord, thou hast searched me, and known me.
Thou knowest my downsitting and mine uprising, thou
understandest my thought afar off.
Thou compassest my path and my lying down, and art acquainted
with all my ways.
For there is not a word in my tongue, but, lo, O Lord, thou knowest it
altogether.
Thou hast beset me behind and before, and laid thine hand upon me.
Such knowledge is too wonderful for me; it is high, I cannot attain
unto it.

I believe these words should not be understood too easily as merely comforting and pleasant. For it can also entail a certain responsibility or be threatening to realize that the other person actually knows you better than you do. It takes the whole psalm before the poet surrenders himself to this omniscient being and accepts Him:

Search me, O God, and know my heart: try me, and know my
thoughts:
And see if there be any wicked way in me, and lead me in the way
everlasting.

IV GREEK AND CHRISTIAN

As we have seen in the previous chapters, virtue ethics as we know it originates from ancient Greece. There are interesting parallels to be found in the more or less simultaneous culture of Confucianism in China and Buddhism in India. In this chapter I will only follow the European route, which leads from Greece to Rome and the rest of Europe. In the Roman Empire, Greek culture was Latinized: as we shall see, this translation into Latin had major consequences. Its beginnings can be traced back to the period of Hellenism, that is to say, roughly between 250 BC and AD 250. This indication, beginning with 'AD' (Anno Domini, in the 'year of the Lord'), already indicates how great the influence of Christianity is on the further development of European culture.

The Roman Latinization of Greek culture has at least two sides: on the one hand it remains indebted to that earlier Greek world, whereas on the other hand, and at the same time, it renews and enriches it. The same goes for Christianity: on the one hand it invades an existing culture, but on the other it draws and copies a lot from it. So there are two sides to this Christianization as well: modification and supplementation. Or, rather, by adapting to the ancient culture in which it develops, Christianity will increasingly modify that culture itself. By interpreting ancient culture in the light of the texts and practices of early Christianity, it discovers in that culture elements that antiquity itself had not developed. In this way it renews what it takes over, complements what it depends on, and thus fully realizes what is called 'tradition'. Tradition should be understood as a verb, a verb that refers to a conversation that is going on, in which new participants occasionally join, who start by listening but gradually determine and change the tone of the conversation. In this chapter I will describe some elements of this conversation as far as it takes place in the field of virtue ethics.

The Christianization of the ancient world is a process that extends over many centuries, in many different domains, and in a multitude of ways. Even if we limit ourselves to the domain of virtue ethics and to the period prior to the Reformation in the sixteenth century, that process is far too extensive to discuss within the scope of a chapter. The Christian world was not only often at war, but its theoretical foundation was also divided into conflicting positions. Apart from explicit conflicts – be it wars or disputes – there was, of course, a great variety of interpretations in such a large area and over such a long period of time. Jasmijn Bovendeert writes in the introduction to her dissertation (2007) about two different schools that have existed since early Christianity. On the one hand there is the school of Philo and Clement of Alexandria, and on the other Greek Church Fathers. They tried to explain Holy Scripture within the conceptual framework of Greek Hellenistic philosophy. On the other hand, there is the school of the Latin Church Fathers who entered into direct dialogue with Cicero and his Latin reception of Hellenistic philosophy and especially Stoicism. Within the Latin Western European tradition we can make a further distinction – from the early Middle Ages on – between on the one hand a primarily exegetical tradition in which the four cardinal virtues were found in the Bible, and on the other hand a rather philosophical-theological reception and elaboration of virtue ethics. Although according to Bovendeert the exegetical school is the most important one, I will focus in this chapter on the philosophical-theological reception. Referring to the works of Augustine and Thomas Aquinas, I will show something of the innovations that this Christian reception brings to the ancient thinking about virtues; a renewal that – as I have already suggested in the previous chapter – is too often overlooked by the contemporary philosophy of the art of living well. We will see that the Christianization of virtue ethics took place in at least three ways: the ancient virtues were translated and reinterpreted (section 1), they were differentiated and systematized more than they had been (section 2), and they were supplemented with some new, 'theological' virtues (section 3).

1 Translation and interpretation

First of all, ancient thinking had to be translated. In the literal sense of the word, this work had already started with the Romans and especially with Cicero (106–43 BC). However, the real translation was not yet done with converting the words in another language: the terms that were used had to be reinterpreted. To start with, the context in which Greek authors like Plato and Aristotle had designed their thinking about virtues was different from the context in which later Hellenistic authors developed it further. The Greeks in the city-state of Athens lived differently from the Romans who lived in the centre of a world empire. Still, the difference between the Greek and Roman world on the one hand and early Christianity on the other was even bigger. Aristotle and Cicero were – however different from each other – both politically involved, self-aware aristocrats and their virtuosity breathes the spirit of distinction that goes with it. The new Christian authors, on the other hand, often did not belong to the political elite and were inspired by very different ideals.

We should therefore not downplay the translation work done by Christian authors. It was not so much an existing message that had to be translated into another vocabulary, but interpretation and translation had to be carried out between different cultures, different worlds. Moreover, Christian authors were not primarily concerned with transforming ancient doctrine into a new language, but rather with expressing the 'good news' of the gospel in the terminology of an earlier world, or with revealing the 'actual', higher meaning of the earlier doctrine through its new contextualisation. And these different intentions were regularly mixed with each other. Ambrose (339–397), for example, was born in Trier, the son of a rich and distinguished Roman family, but ended up as the bishop of Milan at a time when Christianity had only recently been accepted in the Roman Empire. About four hundred years after Cicero, he wrote a book with the same title as a famous book by Cicero: *De officiis*, literally *On Duties*. This term 'duties' should not be misunderstood: in fact, the book is about virtues and about guidelines for a virtuous life. Just as Cicero focused mainly on the education of the distinguished citizens, Ambrose had the leading figures among Christians in mind. To this day the question is still being discussed whether Ambrose tried to give authority to the Christian message by reformulating it in the words of the ancient tradition, or whether he wanted to 'redefine' the ancient tradition in a higher meaning derived from Christianity. Was his book an attempt to reconcile both traditions or did Ambrose use the title to replace Cicero's text by his own (Bovendeert 2007: 40)? Presumably, Ambrose will have had a bit of both these intentions.

Another example of this author's pretensions, and one in which the drastic character of the Christian 'translation' of the ancient virtues is shown, can be found in the eulogy Ambrose wrote for his brother Satyrus,

De excessu fratris Satyri. He used a classical pattern and, just like the Romans, structured this speech in which the deceased was to be praised with the help of the four virtues that already appear as the principal four in Plato's work: (1) wisdom (*phronèsis*), (2) courage (*andreia*), (3) temperance (*sophrosyne*) and (4) justice (*dikaiosynè*). Ambrose then described these four virtues in a Christian sense, so they would obtain a new meaning and describe the characteristics of a Christian life: (1) *prudentia* concerns the love of God, (2) *fortitudo* is the virtue of the martyr, (3) *temperantia* is connected to typically Christian virtues such as reservedness and chastity, and (4) *iustitia* is equated with charity (Bovendeert 2007: 68).

Ambrose became an important teacher to Augustine (354–430), after the latter had left Rome for Milan, which was the imperial residence at the time. Two years after moving to Milan, Augustine converted to Christianity and was baptized by Ambrose. Augustine had been interested in Greek philosophy for a long time. He was particularly familiar with Neoplatonism and with the many Hellenistic schools in which the art of living well and religion were strongly mixed (especially in Manicheism).

After all, in the Hellenistic period philosophy was, in the words of Hadot, 'a way of life' (cf. Chapter III.2.1). Augustine probably knew Aristotle, the most important ancient author on virtues, only through the works of Cicero. Partly because of this, Augustine's significance for the development of virtue ethics lies not so much in the translation and interpretation of Greek tradition into a new context, but rather in the renewal of that tradition through the introduction of new elements. I will describe how that happened a bit further on. Now, I will first jump a few hundred years ahead in time, to show a little bit more about the first way in which Christianity mixed with ancient culture and changed it, namely through the work of translation and interpretation.

How extensive and far-reaching that translational work was and what can happen in such a translation, we see most clearly in Thomas Aquinas (1225–74). Dutch philosopher Marcel Becker showed extensively, in his dissertation (1997), how the virtue of courage, which to Aristotle was the ultimate virtue for the battlefield and thus for soldiers, becomes the virtue of the martyr in Aquinas's work. I will now elaborate on another example: the way in which Thomas Aquinas deals with the Aristotelian virtues that govern our attitude towards property and possessions. We will see why here too the translation into a new context has far-reaching consequences.

The subject is discussed in several places in Aristotle's *Ethics*. In the book devoted to justice, Aristotle distinguishes different meanings of that concept. To the extent that it is a moral virtue in the strict sense, justice consists of wanting to have as much as a just law determines; that is, to have as much as one is entitled to, no more and no less. Although Aristotle believes virtue is a middle between two extremes, and we should indeed speak of 'no more and no less', he himself only explicitly mentions *one* of the extremes here. For Aristotle there is only the vice of wanting more than you deserve: the *pleonexia* (*Ethics*, 1129b). The opposite extreme, 'wanting to have less than you deserve', is apparently too unlikely for him to mention.

In book IV of his *Nicomachean Ethics* – prior to and separately from the discussion of justice – two other virtues were already discussed in connection with dealing with property and ownership (*Ethics*, 1120a–1122b). Neither *eleutheria* (generosity) nor *megaloprepeia* ('grandezza' or magnificence) relate to the way in which we acquire, own and guard property, but rather to the way in which we use it, that is, spend it. The best way to do this is to know how to spend on those to whom it is appropriate, in the appropriate quantity and at the right time. To do that, and to do it from a virtuous attitude, and thus easily and with pleasure, it is necessary for you not to be too attached to your possessions. Those who are too concerned about their money to be able to spend it freely are not free and not generous (*aneleutheriotès*). The opposite vice, having too little concern for what you have, is again not very likely according to Aristotle; he calls it foolish rather than bad and it is easy to cure, according to him. The *megaloprepeia* is actually the same virtue as the *eleutheria*, but 'in large', that is: for people who have a lot of money to spend.

Two things stand out in Aristotle's discussion of the theme. First, as said, the idea of finding the middle between two extremes doesn't work very well with regard to these virtues. Only in connection to *megaloprepeia* does Aristotle succeed in mentioning two opposing vices: *banausia* or ostentation and *mikroprepeia* or the fear of spending too much. Second, apart from this there is something else remarkable in Aristotle's treatment of virtuous spending: it is always more about the giver than about the one to whom is given. Generosity and magnificence adorn the virtuous man, they seem to be intended more in perfection of the virtuous than in aid of the needy to whom something is given. In the 'translation' of these virtues by Thomas Aquinas, these peculiarities each get an interesting twist.

Aquinas did not read Greek himself and therefore did not translate it in a strict sense. He used the translation that his fellow brother Willem van Moerbeke made of the writings of Aristotle, including *Ethics*, at his request. In Moerbeke's translation justice appears as *iustitia*, and the other two virtues mentioned (*eleutheria* and *megaloprepeia*) are translated as *liberalitas* and *magnificentia* respectively. In Aquinas's use of that translation, however, a more important further 'translation' takes place.

First, Aquinas states that the latter two virtues, the two types of generosity, are not exclusively reserved for those who have (a lot of) money. While Aristotle clearly has the wealthy bourgeoisie in mind, Aquinas explicitly says that the poor can also be *liberalis* (generous) and even *magnificens* (magnanimous) (STh, IIaIIae 117.1–3 and 134.3–4). This is possible because Aquinas makes it clear from the outset that these virtues are not so much about the external act, but about the inner choice. They are a moderation of the inner desire for and attachment to possession (STh, IIaIIae 117.1–3). It is true that with Aristotle, too, virtue exists in a well-cultivated desire, but the Greek citizen was much more focused on what 'virtuous action' looks like than the Christian medieval thinker (and certainly the monk).

Second, unlike Aristotle, Aquinas does pay attention to the person who receives something, in two ways. First of all, according to him, generosity functions in service of Christian charity (*caritas*), and since one's neighbour is the receiver, he gets more attention (STh, IIaIIae 118.1–2 and 123.12–15). Next and above all, Aquinas – again in contrast to Aristotle – treats *liberalitas* and *magnificentia* explicitly as being connected with the cardinal virtue of justice; and this connection fundamentally consists in giving each as he deserves (STh, IIaIIae 58.11). According to Aquinas, the thing a person rightfully deserves is what he needs. He who has more than he needs, keeps it from others. Actually I shouldn't say 'who *has* more', but 'who *uses* more' than he needs. Riches (abundant possessions) are not the problem according to Aquinas – as long as they are used to serve those who need them. So with Aquinas, generosity is no longer primarily a question of a way of life in which the noble shows his moral quality, but it is obedience to a demand of justice, in which justice is done to the other. I will come back to the important role of justice (in section 3.3 of this chapter).

Third, the attitude that was too unlikely for Aristotle to be mentioned, namely 'wanting less than you deserve', Aquinas certainly deems possible. The Christian religious orders knew the vow of poverty, which as a Dominican friar Aquinas himself had made. Instead of interpreting this vow as a faulty extreme, Aquinas elevates this deliberately chosen poverty to a virtue, albeit one that cannot be asked of everyone (STh, IIaIIae

185.6). Sometimes it seems as if he interprets *magnificentia*, which is the superlative of *liberalitas*, as this voluntary poverty (ScG, III 134.7). That would reconnect it with justice, the effect of which – as we have already seen – is *magnificentia*. Elsewhere, however, it becomes clear that this voluntary poverty is in two ways a perfection of the new virtue that Christianity will introduce: *caritas* (see section 3.3). First, a total renunciation of property means greater freedom for the love of God and neighbour; and second, voluntary poverty in monastic life means that one has only common property, and thus takes care of one another even with regard to property (ScG, III 135.5; STh, IIaIIae 188.7). The interpretation of generous giving as a form of love reinforces, again, the focus on the other in virtuous giving. This idea of love, *caritas*, does not occur at all in Aristotle. We will see (in section 3) that it is one of the new elements that was later added in the history of classical virtue ethics. In this addition, Augustine will prove to play an important role.

In this section we saw that Aquinas's explanation of the Aristotelian doctrine of virtues – even disregarding such new additions and without ever criticizing 'the philosopher' (as he usually calls Aristotle) – introduces many new elements. This already happens because he translates and interprets Aristotle's aristocratic ethics in such a way that they also appear to fit with, and clarify, the Christian life of ordinary people. This first aspect of the Christianization of virtue ethics is not only important for an adequate picture of history. It also teaches us what to do if we want to update virtue ethics for our time. This is not a question of simply applying the old virtues to contemporary problems: they will have to be translated and interpreted and therefore renewed. This requires that we translate the Aristotelian virtues into contemporary words and that we learn to interpret our own time in terms of those virtues.

For us, the differences between rich and poor exist more on a global scale than they do locally. This inevitably changes the nature of giving. We hardly see (or only through all kinds of mediations, from news items on television to begging letters) to whom we give or what the result is; and the recipient sees even less of us. However, the connection between the virtue of giving and the virtue of justice does not become less important. Aristotle describes generosity as an example of the excellence of the virtuous self, and wanting to have more than you deserve as a form of injustice. For Aquinas, giving is in any case primarily a question of justice and it only turns into charity if it becomes as radical as the self-chosen poverty. Perhaps it is misleading if, in our time, much of our 'aid to poor and underdeveloped countries' is seen as charity – not to mention 'left-wing hobbies', as far-right politicians like to call it. The tradition of virtue ethics suggests that development aid is not about giving, but rather about *giving back* and about correcting unjust distributions.

For Aristotle, the difference between rich and poor was an unproblematic starting point. For us, however, it no longer is; not because the differences in our society are smaller than they were in his, but because nowadays we demand more equality. In the context of our globalized world, the differences between rich and poor are terrible: even within Europe's borders, the richest earn many times more than the poorest, even if the figures are corrected for extreme peaks; in the OECD (Organisation for Economic Co-operation and Development) countries, the richest 20 per cent earn more than nine times as much as the poorest 20 per cent. On a global scale, the ratio is even more skewed: 20 per cent of the world's population accounts for more than 80 per cent of consumption. The gap between the rich and the poor has widened in almost all (relatively rich) OECD countries over the last twenty-five years. In such circumstances, finding the right balance (how much, for the benefit of whom, at what time?) becomes more difficult and more important. It is evident that the notorious top salaries and bonuses are both excessive and shameful. It is actually equally clear, but more difficult to acknowledge, that we who are among the richest on earth are in a certain sense all guilty of indulgence and injustice. Moreover, it is less clear what would be the right balance. Some philosophers have argued why we should be obliged to give at least one-tenth of our income to the poor. The fact that such a limited measure, which would leave so much inequality in existence, is still so far from being realized, again gives a poignant picture of our situation. The idea of the equal dignity of every human being, which Aristotle did not yet know, makes equality in payment a stronger demand, and tolerating great inequality a greater scandal.

The middle between avarice and profligacy, or between niggardliness and boastfulness, cannot simply be transplanted from ancient Athenian society to our contemporary society of abundance. Moreover, it is more difficult to reach that middle if you are pulled so strongly to one extreme, as is the case in our capitalist economy, which is based on overconsumption. If we do not buy more than we need, paradoxically we all become poorer. According to the experts, an equal distribution of all goods and profits would also generate poverty. That means that we – more than Aristotle and Thomas Aquinas – will have to think about *how* we give. It is clear that a translation of the classical tradition is constantly needed and cannot be made once and for all, and that such a translation is not an easy task.

2 Differentiating and arranging

The second way in which the Christianization of virtues has had an impact on the development of virtue ethics is by no means separate from the translation work discussed so far. Every translator knows from experience that different aspects of the word that has to be translated actually require different new terms. What one language says in one word can only be described by different words in another language; the meaning of the initial word is then divided into several words. The thought that expresses itself in the language is thus differentiated by the work of translation. This greater differentiation in turn requires a systematization that makes it clear how the different terms and concepts are interwoven.

We can already see that happening in the first major translation in the history of virtue ethics, as it was provided by the Romans and in which Cicero in particular played a major role. The meaning and influence of a translation in general, and of its translation of the Greek virtues in particular, can be illustrated by the cardinal virtue called *sophrosyne* in Greek, which I described earlier as 'temperance'. Cicero needs several words for this, including *temperantia, continentia, moderatio, modestia* (see for example *De Officiis* III.116). Apparently, this typically Greek term could not be translated completely into a single Latin term. Its meaning includes 'austerity' or 'frugality' as well as 'modesty', 'mildness', 'self-control', 'uniformity' and 'stability', as well as 'temperance' or 'proportionality'. Such a multitude of meanings requires a concept in which this diversity is captured and which makes it clear why they are all forms of one and the same virtue. In the case of *sophrosyne* it is clearly about an arranging virtue, in which that which must be arranged in one way or another is 'multiple' and 'diverse', with all the tension that goes with it. Multiplicity and diversity can relate to anything: desires, passions, emotions and judgements. They all have to be ordered both in relation to each other and in themselves. Moreover, they can each be differentiated individually: we long for pleasure, possession, power and recognition.

And in all these areas we can be excessive, that is to say: sacrifice everything in favour of a single desire or a single object. The task is to find the right balance. Multiplicity requires restraint and control, but also an understanding of the various interests, desires and possibilities. The Greek term for the virtue of temperance is etymologically interpreted as 'sound-mindedness': *sophrosyne* was the name for the ability to balance those many interests, desires and emotions. I need not explain why it is one of the cardinal virtues.

For the Greeks, this virtue was mainly about the desire to enjoy eating and drinking and sex. However, the translation into Latin makes it clear that this virtue has a much wider scope. A translation that tries to do justice to as many connotations of the concept as possible, inevitably fans out in a variety of terms. And of course this multiplication of terms requires an interpretation that explains the inner connections, and thus leads to a systematization as we indeed find in Cicero. In Book I of *De Officiis* he arranges the many virtues in a scheme of four sources of 'moral rectitude', i.e. of that 'quod est honestum' (I.15). The fourth part in fact concerns the virtues that can be summarized under the concept of temperance (I.93), which are then further differentiated and ordered by Cicero (I.100).

Such systematic organization is more necessary as the number of virtues increases. This number increases not only because of the translation, but also because of the application of virtue ethics in the *praxis* of life. As the virtues are used more frequently for moral education, the elementary categories of the first theorists will be developed according to their specific meaning for different domains of human life. While Aristotle distinguishes only a dozen moral virtues and five intellectual virtues in his *Ethics*, over the course of time many dozens of virtues are distinguished. And as the number grows, so does the need for order. This development of differentiation and systematization is clearly reflected in the Christian authors. Jasmijn Bovendeert (2007: 48–54) shows how this happens with Ambrose. I will limit myself to a few examples from the ethical part of Thomas Aquinas's *Summa Theologica*: the *quaestiones* 47 to 170 from the *secunda secundae* (STh, IIaIIae 47–170).

It will not come as a surprise that the four cardinal virtues – courage, temperance, prudence and justice – play an important role in the systematizing process. These already offer a first subdivision, and moreover one that has been given authority by a long tradition – they are already listed by Plato (*Politeia*, 427e). Aquinas now makes it clear that this scheme needs to be further elaborated. For something can be subdivided in three different ways: (1) by its necessary components (as the foundation, walls and roof are the necessary components of a house), (2) by their types (as huts, houses, apartments and palaces are different types of dwellings), and (3) by the additional components, possible effects or applications of something in different domains (a house can have a barn; a house can be an official residence, a temporary residence or a family property, etc.). By further differentiating the four cardinal virtues using these three types of divisions, Aquinas develops a scheme in which he can order many virtues and give each one its own place.

The virtue of *temperance* has as its constituents (1) diffidence or shame and the sense of honour or feeling for what is appropriate. As kinds of temperance (2), Aquinas differentiates abstinence and sobriety with regard to food and drink, and chastity and virginity with regard to sexuality. As (3) possible effects of temperance he mentions self-control, meekness, clemency and modesty. The latter itself can be divided into humility and studiousness, which is the desirable middle between unrestrained curiosity and disinterest.

The virtue of *courage* is constituted by (1) a power that is necessary to come to courageous action, and to subsequently sustain it. Each of them comes in different kinds (2): confidence and magnificence (conceived as a kind of ambition); and next to that patience or strength and perseverance. The effects of it (3) can be distinguished according to whether they relate to more or less opposition and greater or lesser dangers.

The virtue of *justice* has the most subdivisions, which confirms its status of supreme virtue. As components (1) – which are both necessary, but which can nevertheless be distinguished – Aquinas mentions on the one hand the avoidance of evil and on the other hand the doing of good. As kinds (2) he distinguishes distributive and commutative (or restorative) justice. The latter is subdivided according to whether it concerns voluntary transactions (buying, selling and borrowing) or involuntary (robbery and other forms of damaging). These 'involuntary transactions' can exist in actions as well as in words; in the first case it is about respecting the life, physical integrity and possessions of other people; in the second case it is about the righteous judgement and respectful treatment of others. The possible effects (3) of justice are distinguished according to the person to whom or the thing to which 'justice is done'. For example, according to Aquinas, doing justice to God requires the virtue of worship. Doing justice to people can be subdivided according to whether it concerns all people or particular persons: the attitude that does justice to the special obligations you have towards relatives, we call *piety*. The relationship with higher-ranking individuals requires respect, dedication and obedience. Gratitude is appropriate to the one who is kind to us; truthfulness and kindness to all, and generosity and fairness to those who depend on us.

The virtue of *prudence* (which Aquinas treats first, because it is required for the other virtues), too, can be divided into other, new virtues. Its components (1) are memory, open-mindedness, intelligence, shrewdness, rationality, foresight, circumspection and caution. Aquinas then distinguishes different kinds (2) on the basis of the fact that prudence exists not only with regard to one's own affairs, but also with regard to family affairs, military affairs and political issues; and with regard to the latter, a distinction can be made between prudence for the politician and for the citizen. As additional virtues (3) Aquinas finally mentions deliberating, judging and commanding.

In this way an impressive structure of virtues is created. From the Middle Ages onwards, this is also reflected in the iconography: the system of virtues is represented in towers and castles in which the relationship between the different parts and the relationship between 'foundation' and 'extension' becomes clear. In Aquinas's elaboration of the cardinal virtues, the influence of typically Christian elements – such as humility and the care for others – is clear. But these elements, as well as explicitly religious virtues (such as the worship of God), do not break through the classical pattern of virtue ethics with its emphasis on what is appropriate, its doctrine of the desirable middle and its cardinal virtues. On the contrary: the Christian elements seem to be organically incorporated into it.

In contemporary elaborations of virtue ethics there is much less emphasis on systematization, but the same kind of differentiation can still easily be recognized. In *The Family Virtues Guide* (Popov 1997) a publication for primary education, no less than fifty-two virtues are distinguished, including typically contemporary virtues such as assertiveness and flexibility. In his *A Short Treatise on the Great Virtues*, André Comte-Sponville (2002) describes eighteen different virtues, and within one of them, love, he distinguishes three types. The reception of ancient virtue ethics in the Christian Middle Ages provides an instructive example of what has to be done again and again in every age: the virtues have to be differentiated according to their meaning for different aspects of life and with the help of the contemporary understanding of human action.

3 Addition

The application of ancient virtues requires translation and differentiation. This applies not only to Christianity, but to every new time and context. However, there is also a radical new element that Christianity brings into or adds to virtue ethics. This new element has to do with the typically Christian elements I mentioned earlier: poverty, humility and care for others. Something resounds here that, in a way, does not fit in at all with classical virtue ethics. According to Aristotle, virtue is the way in which a person can make his life succeed. Life is about happiness, which is realized in an optimally developed life that gets the recognition it deserves. Virtues are the hallmarks of a successful life. That is why examples play such an important role: everyone recognizes a virtuous person as the one who has succeeded in what everyone actually strives for. As said (Chapter III.1): classical virtue ethics is a form of ethics that is in line with human desire. The upbringing that goes with it is one of cultivation: people naturally long for the good, they only need to be shaped and trained to ensure that they also acquire an adequate understanding of the good and practice to make them realize it 'by nature'. Being virtuous is a second nature, distinguished from, but in continuity with and as a perfection of our 'first nature', so to speak. It is true that this cultivation needs a certain education as help, but that help is only aimed at the pupil's realization of that which he or she already strives for. Aristotelian virtue ethics is an ethics of self-realization; the virtuous person is the one who is successful, and in that sense is happy. And as mentioned earlier (Chapter III.3), the Hellenistic philosophy of Stoicism stresses the link between virtue and happiness even more.

Virtues such as humility and caring for others do not fit into that image easily. According to Aristotle, too, a virtuous person will be focused on the welfare of those with whom he or she forms a community. However, this is important to him primarily because the well-being of his or her community also determines his or her own happiness. Which means that others only count as far as I am connected to them, as far as their happiness determines my happiness. Even if we understand this broadly – in our time the world has become a global village; in the news we are confronted with all the misery in the world – it remains something different from what Christianity seems to say, which is that *everyone* is 'my neighbour'. Christianity makes this even worse by pointing out as examples the sick, the hungry, the outcast, that is to say: those whom we prefer to overlook. For Aristotle, humility is as much a vice as conceit. Between these two extremes lies the virtuous middle of the one who knows what he or she is worth, who is reasonably responsible (EN, 1125b). Caring for others outside the circle of my community, focusing on the other as another person, renouncing one's own success in the service of the other – that does not fit within the Aristotelian framework. It is precisely these things, however, that are essential to Christian morality.

Does this mean that Christian morality is not about happiness and the way in which it is realized through virtue? Sometimes that appears to be the case; for example, when Augustine in *The City of God* (Book V.20) distances himself from all kinds of philosophical-ethical positions that can all be called 'eudaimonistic', because they are aimed at happiness (*eudaimonia*). He distances himself from the Stoics who identify happiness with virtue and localize the highest human good in virtue; from the Epicureans, who see happiness as pleasure and standardize virtue by the extent to which it contributes to bodily pleasure, which for them is the highest good; from those (presumably Aristotelians) according to whom happiness consists in recognition and who portray virtues as 'slaves of human glory'; and also from the cynics, for whom happiness exists in the absence of pain and who therefore seek detachment and pretend to be 'despisers of glory' and 'disregard the judgement of other men, seem to themselves wise, and please themselves'. All these positions – which only differ in the fact that they give a different interpretation to *eudaimonia* – are opposed by Augustine to the attitude he presents as ideal.

> [H]e who, with true piety towards God, whom he loves, believes, and hopes in, fixes his attention more on those things in which he displeases himself, than on those things, if there are any such, which please himself, or rather, not himself, but the truth, does not attribute that by which he can now please the truth to anything but to the mercy of Him whom he has feared to displease (Augustine, *The City of God*, Book V.20)

This passage contains at least three elements that are important for an explanation of what Christianity adds to classical virtue ethics. I will mention and discuss them in reverse order: (1) instead of the self-activity of self-realization, the activity of God now comes first; (2) instead of the focus on success, attention to failure now plays a major role; and (3) instead of the classical virtues, three new qualities appear: faith, hope and love. Remarkably, these three are also called 'virtues', but of a different kind. Apparently even in this Christian 'correction' or 'addition' to virtue ethics it is still about virtues! Indeed, even these virtues fit into an ethical theory that is focused on happiness. However, Christianity teaches that besides the happiness of a successful life, there is another, 'higher' form of happiness. Thomas Aquinas starts the ethical part of his *Summa Theologica* (IaIIae 5.5), just like Aristotle, with a reflection on the highest good. Just like Aristotle, he too defines happiness as the highest good. However, according to Aquinas, happiness consists of two elements: there is 'earthly' happiness that exists in (natural) virtue, and there is the eternal happiness that exists in seeing God. The other virtues would give a taste of the latter. What does this mean? Let us examine what this expansion of virtue ethics consists of, how it has an effect (for these new virtues will also permeate and change the 'natural' virtues, and the associated conception of earthly happiness) and, above all, what we, today, in our secular time, have to do with them.

3.1 'In us, without us'

Aristotelian virtue ethics is an ethics of self-realization. This does not only mean that its purpose, happiness, consists in a perfectly developed self, but also that we should realize this by ourselves. While virtues are acquired through upbringing ('character virtues') and education ('intellectual virtues'), the participation of the individual is also crucial in this respect. Upbringing cannot make a person virtuous if he or she does not make an effort himself, nor can education give a person insight if he or she does not think for him- or herself. Becoming virtuous, and the happiness that comes with it, may presuppose an environment or a community that helps you, but it is ultimately the merit of the virtuous self.

If we compare this with the definition which – according to Thomas Aquinas – Augustine gives of virtue and which he himself adopts, we see a remarkable difference. Aquinas wrote: 'Virtue is a good quality of the mind, by which we live righteously, of which no one can make bad use, which God works in us, without us' (STh, IIaIIae 55.4,1). Although the explanation given by Aquinas fits with Aristotle's definition of virtue, this certainly does not apply to his conclusion: virtue is created by God, 'in us, without us'. Aristotle obviously does not speak of God as Aquinas does, but he also strongly resists an extra- or supernatural interpretation of virtue: it is – according to Aristotle – through custom and practice that a natural talent can develop into virtue (EN, 1103a, 20vv). Through every action we take, we define ourselves: we create a model, which we use the next time we encounter a similar situation. As we act more often in a particular way, we develop a habit, and from that, the disposition (suitability and propensity) to act in that way grows. If that disposition is good, we call it a virtue.

For Augustine, nature had fallen too far and humans were too dependent on the grace of God to enable such an ethic of self-realization. If humans could be good at all, then it is only thanks to a blessing from God. And someone who does not recognize this indebtedness is, because of that, not virtuous, for he or she is overconfident and unjustly relying on his own abilities. A truly virtuous person, as we have already seen in the quotation from *The City of God*, does not attribute the things through which he or she can please to his or her own excellence, but exclusively to the mercy of Him to whom he or she fears to offend.

For us that sounds strange, incomprehensible even. But it is problematic for Thomas Aquinas too: Aristotle's authority is inviolable to him, but he cannot challenge the Church Father Augustine either. His solution is typical of the reconciliatory genius that characterizes him: Augustine is right, but only for a certain category of virtues, namely the Christian or theological virtues. In addition to the (Aristotelian) virtues that we acquire through our own activity, there are other virtues that we cannot acquire ourselves, but only receive. Aquinas then connects these two kinds of virtues with each other by saying that the virtues caused in us by God also presuppose action on our part, and that the virtues that we have established ourselves cannot be realized without God (STh, IIaIIae 55.4–6). Can Aquinas's solution help us? What can we do, what should we do with virtues we cannot form ourselves, but can only receive?

To answer that question, we first need to better understand why Augustine came up with such a claim. The context of the definition of virtue attributed to him is important here: human nature is a fallen nature. Through the Fall, the revolt against God, nature has lost its innocence and integrity. These theological words capture an experience we all know, but of which we missed the recognition in the contemporary philosophy of the art of living well: the experience of evil, of human error, of failure. A further elaboration this brings us to the second characteristic element of the Christian addition to virtue ethics.

3.2 The evil of sin

Of course the Greeks also knew that people can fail and that they usually do so. Aristotle points out that ethics is just like archery: there are many possibilities to miss the target, and only one to shoot in the middle of the boss. That does not mean that everything that is not perfect is wrong. On the contrary: even in good things, ever greater perfection is possible. Improvements starts with recognizing the imperfection of what we have achieved. Nevertheless, Christianity will bring in an important new element in culture and virtue ethics.

Classical Greek virtue ethics is (as said in Chapter III.1) a form of ethics 'in line with the (natural) desire'. We have to realize that it arises in a context that has a much greater confidence in (human) nature than is evident to us. Natural reality as a whole, the cosmos, is seen as a good and beautiful order (the Greek word *kosmos* actually means 'jewel'). Human nature is, at least in principle, likewise 'in order'. People then strive for the optimal realization and development of the good that has already been given in the bud. The thing we should do is exactly what we actually want to do, and what we are in fact already aiming for. In addition, we are also by nature capable of realizing what we are aiming for. Just as an artefact (Plato usually uses the pruning blade as an example) is best suited to do that, what it is meant to do and what it is supposed to do (i.e. pruning), the same goes for nature. A plant is naturally suited for and aimed at full bloom and development. And for humans, what we 'should do' is the same as what we 'actually' want and what our nature enables us to do. These days, to us, this sounds too good to be true – and that shows that we, whether we like it or not, whether we are religious or not, are all influenced through and through by this renewal that began with Christianity.

Even Aristotle acknowledges that the reality of human action is often not as beautiful as this scheme suggests. Ethics would not even be necessary if we all did all the right things by ourselves. Sometimes things go wrong in nature. The way Aristotle (just like other authors of antiquity) understands this failure is illustrative of the distance that exists between him and us.

Just as a plant can be disturbed in its growth and can wither due to the wrong circumstances, so too can a human also be distorted. For example, we can develop a wrong image of happiness – as if it exists in pleasure or fame or something else. The community in which a person is raised determines to a large extent his or her ideas of the good life and the examples in which he or she recognizes it. Natural desires can remain uncultivated, for example when they never meet a higher quality: anyone who always has his headphones on will never discover the beneficial effects of silence. Due to all kinds of circumstances, the ability to direct and shape one's own natural abilities can remain underdeveloped. Some people never develop the strength to actually commit themselves to what they intend to do. Those who have never learned to hold back will be more easily blinded and let themselves go: one is not born with a 'short fuse'. Aristotelian ethics is an ethics of training and education par excellence. All these examples of unsuccessful development, of deformation, actually point more to 'imperfection' than to what we would call moral 'evil'. In Aristotle's case, the one who is not virtuous always resembles either someone who is mistaken, or someone who is too inexperienced and unformed to succeed in what he or she strives for. Acting wrong is more like 'missing a goal' than what we would call moral evil. I already referred to the example of the archer that Aristotle likes to use: a very good one almost always hits his target; the less trained one will easily shoot next to it. It is ultimately all a matter of talent, practice and a little bit of luck.

For us, on the other hand, 'evil' is not so much 'less good', but the opposite of good; and not so much a question of bad luck or lack of understanding or practice, but something much more serious. Someone who does evil is not mistaken in what he or she wants, but wants something wrong. Of course, the Greeks also knew this more serious evil: their tragedies are filled with examples of murder and manslaughter. Although it is usually not humans who act themselves, but fate that seizes them, or some god or daemon – think of how Ajax or Medea are blinded by hatred or feelings of revenge, so that they themselves become victims as much as the perpetrators of the evil they do.

It is probably due to the introduction of Christianity (and thus of a Semitic tradition) into European culture that we have discovered that we are less 'innocent' and that nature is less perfect than Greek ethics suggests. The myths of the Fall of Man (Gen. 3) and of the War in Heaven show a very different understanding of evil. Evil in this case is rather the expression of a fundamental (human) desire that is the opposite of the desire for good. In its extreme form evil can become 'diabolical', like a devil that dominates the good. The conflict between God and the devil is a representation of the dualistic scheme that this conception of evil always bears witness to. This dualism can be more or less radical and can take different forms: as a struggle between body and mind ('the spirit is willing, but the flesh is weak'; Mt. 26.41), between nature and reason (in Kant's work it is called respectively 'inclination' and 'duty'), between different forces inside of us ('Zwei Seelen wohnen, ach! in meiner Brust', says Goethe's Faust: I.1112), between selfishness and altruism, and so on.

Augustine, who plays such an important role in the Christianization of virtues, does not want – after his Manichaean period – to speak of a dualism of two forces, but of a struggle between two opposing tendencies in the will itself: a struggle that makes me want and *not* want something at the same time, 'a struggle of myself against myself'. At least, this is how he explains in his *Confessions* (VIII: sections 22–7) his doubt about whether or not he should be baptized. Some authors have claimed that in this conflict, the will itself is revealed as a capacity that the Greeks did not yet know, and about which the philosophers of the art of living well once again seem to speak too easily. In the previous chapter we saw that they put all the emphasis on discovering what you actually want, choosing to do so and realizing it. But if you think that living a good life is only a matter of knowing what you want, you may not know what that actually is, the 'will'.

Not only through his doubt, but also, and above all, through the experience of evil, Augustine discovers the will as that remarkable faculty that distinguishes itself from both desire and reason and that can be set against both. Unlike the other two, will does not, in fact, have a natural tendency towards its own 'good'. Reason naturally seeks insight and thus truth. When you think, you try to gain true insight; you cannot reasonably try to make a mistake. Lust or desire naturally strives for pleasure; and if nature is not distorted, this pleasure is good as well. In the wild no animal will try to eat what is bad for its health. If people do, it is a question of distortion. But what could be the natural good regarding the will, that faculty by which we can choose, for example whether we follow our desire or reason? By itself, it aims for nothing, unless perhaps for self-assertion. Think of children who at a certain age become stubborn and resist helping hands of parents or others: 'No! I want to do it myself.' We then say they are starting to have a will of their own. The will seems to be that faculty by which we confirm ourselves. In doing so, the will may have a purpose, but it has no content. Its indefinite content not only creates a possibility for doubt (wanting and not wanting something at the same time), but also for evil. For we achieve this self-assertion in particular or at least in the first place by saying 'no', 'no' to that which seems to push or steer us; that is to say, by going against the direction or the commandment of reason and against the insistence of desire. This will – which itself does not seem to have a natural tendency, apart from the desire for rebellion against whatever is held up as a rule or law – is capable of the other, more radical evil that the Semitic tradition shows us. This kind of evil consists in sometimes deliberately doing what is not good, without any good reasons, and without gaining anything from it. Augustine gives the famous example of the pear theft in his youth (*Confessions*, II: section 9). He stole pears without being interested in them; he did not eat them but threw them away. The only motive was the fact that it was forbidden, and the will to break this rule. French writer Nathalie Sarraute (2013) describes an anecdote from her childhood: as she was fantasizing about destroying a leather sofa in a hotel lounge with a pair of scissors, she hears the order of her (German-speaking) babysitter ('Nein, das tust du nicht!') and therefore feels even more strongly the irresistible urge to exceed that order. The hissing sound of the ban not only gives a premonition of the sound that the scissors will make when the leather is cut open, it also alludes to the speaking of the snake in Paradise.

There are more serious examples than this, even if it is not easy to find pure cases of this evil. The enjoyment of the offence is often mixed with the pleasure of its outcome, and the evil of the offence will often be reasoned away with more or less apparent legitimations. The decadent novel *Against the Grain* by J.-K. Huysmans (1969) gives the example of someone who knowingly and deliberately seduces a poor boy to acts that will gradually make him addicted and criminal: 'I shall have contributed, as far as in me lay, to create a scoundrel', and then follows the 'legitimation': 'an enemy to more for the odious society that wrings so heavy a ransom from us all' (Huysmans 1969: 69). The fantasies of the Marquis de Sade not only illustrate the effect of such legitimations, but also show that revolt can be mixed with the affirmation of elementary desires. The evil of wrongdoing can even be mixed with the desire for a real good. Literature provides countless examples that show that the impossibility of love is an extra challenge to realize it. At one and the same time, not only the institution of marriage, but also the faithfulness, the trust and the loyalty that are inevitably presupposed in the intimacy of a love affair, can form a boundary that provokes transgression. The evil of revolt rarely exists in pure form.

The Christian tradition calls this evil, which consists in transgression, the evil of sin. The apostle Paul writes that we only know sin through the law: 'I had not known sin, but by the law: for I had not known lust, except the law had said, 'Thou shalt not covet' (Rom. 7.7). This discovery, that the will can turn against the good and that evil can mix with the good we naturally desire, has consequences for virtue ethics, for an ethics that understands virtue 'in line with the desire'!

And yet virtue ethics, in the history of morality, has survived the introduction of the will and the evil that this will is capable of. Even after the European has lost his or her innocence, the moral ideal still demands virtue. However, it is no longer possible to be virtuous in the same way now, after it has been discovered that evil does not only exist as an error or as the failure of a good pursuit in itself, but also as an offence or revolt, as the action of a resistance to the pursuit of goodness. We have already seen the answer: virtue is still what it is all about, but it is no longer 'in our own hands'.

Besides the virtues we can acquire ourselves, there are the virtues we can only receive. And now we can understand why these new virtues are not the perfection of natural desire or natural reason, but of will. To perfect the will, this faculty which by itself seems to be directed at nothing but the affirmation of itself and which therefore experiences every imposed law or rule as a provocation of transgression, requires more than just practice and formation; we need help from outside. Apart from the question of what kind of virtues this might bring, however, the other question that we have asked a few times before now arises again: what can we, secularized people, still do with these kinds of virtues?

3.3 Faith, hope and love

To find an answer to this question, we will start again with the philosopher we have taken as the most important guide in this chapter: Thomas Aquinas. Aquinas, in fact, presents the situation a little less radically than I have done: according to him, the will is itself directed towards the good, and virtue should only perfect it in the direction it already has. Against the background of what I, with the help of Augustine, emphasized about will and evil, we can better understand what he then says, namely that will cannot by itself reach 'the good that goes beyond one's own ability' (Te Velde 1995: 38). The good to which, according to Aquinas, the will is naturally directed, is one's own good. By shaping and cultivating that directedness, you may be able to come to an enlightened self-interest; you may find that if you don't take good care of your surroundings, you also harm yourself. However, this way, the desired good is still bound to its own interests. Something else is needed to get beyond that. For Aquinas this good 'that is beyond the reach of one's own will' is in the first place God Himself. The new virtues, *faith*, *hope* and *love*, are therefore ultimately all directed towards God, and can only be given by God. Perhaps, however, we do not need this strictly theological interpretation to understand what this is all about.

For there is also another form of 'the good that is beyond one's own ability' than God Himself. Even within the human good we can reach ourselves, Aquinas already sees a possibility, namely in justice. As we have already observed several times, one of the characteristic differences between Aristotle and Aquinas is that in Aquinas's work virtue is explicitly oriented towards the other. This applies in the first place to justice, which is reinterpreted and gets an (even) more important role than it already had with Aristotle. We already saw one of the consequences of this (in section 1 of this chapter): virtues such as generosity (*liberalitas* and *magnificentia*) also become forms of justice, which they were not yet for Aristotle. Indeed, justice is more than just taking the other into account for your own benefit. Even if – both within a national and global society – a fairer distribution of money and goods is ultimately beneficial to everyone, whoever redistributes only for his own benefit, we will not really call fair.

However, true justice, and the orientation towards the good of the other that is required for it, is not achieved by cultivating a natural tendency, but must be brought into it by a force other than the natural ability itself. We do not simply become just, we do so because we are guided to this end. In the case of justice, the power that causes it is not so much the grace of God as the power of the legislator. Without the law that binds us, without international treaties that unite us, justice would be limited to the measure of natural sympathy and one's own advantage. Through the law, we respect the rights of others beyond those limits. Although these laws and treaties are, to a large extent, again motivated by self-interest, thanks to the coercion they exert we can already see in the virtue of justice a bit of an example of what theological virtues will show to a greater extent.

Faith

That theological virtues are the perfections of will is perhaps most evident in faith. Although in a certain sense faith is a form of knowing, and therefore seems to be a perfection of the intellect (STh, IIaIIae 4.3), will is also involved in our knowledge of the intellect. The person in question has to agree with what his intellect understands or sees. This agreeing or assenting (Latin: assentire) is an activity of will. We see that for example when people refuse to believe(!) something that is nevertheless obvious. Even though the evidence of global warming is clear, some still refuse to believe that it is. That refusal is an activity of will. This activity becomes most visible if – conversely – consent is given, despite the fact that the mind does not fully see, i.e. if there is no immediate evidence, or compelling arguments, or empirical evidence (STh, IIaIIae 1.4). And that is what happens in faith, according to Aquinas. Faith is to confirm that something is the case, as if you know it while you cannot rationally verify it; it is to agree with what you cannot know through the intellect.

An additional element should be added to this, an element that makes the theological nature of this virtue even more clear. After all, faith (*fides*) is not the same as opinion (*opinio*). To 'consider something to be the case' is also to agree with what I do not really know, but with a certain degree of doubt. Believing, on the other hand, is, at least according to Aquinas, characterized by certainty. Well, to say with certainty something you cannot really know for sure, that is only possible because the will lifts the intellect beyond its natural limitation, and for that purpose the will has to be brought to where it wouldn't go by itself. In faith – according to Aquinas – the intellect agrees with a truth that it does not know itself, but to which it is moved by the will, which is itself moved by the grace of God (STh, IIaIIae 2.9 and 6.1).

Perhaps we can see a secular parallel of this religious faith in the widespread belief in human rights, about which I wrote in Chapter II.4. That people have certain rights and that these rights go back to a human dignity that is called 'inherent' and 'inalienable' is hardly a form of normal 'knowledge'. The facts rather speak against this. To call this dignity inviolable and absolute suggests a form of certainty more akin to that of faith than to that of any form of scientific knowledge. The example can also make clear how this form of certainty does not rule out doubt, but rather includes it. We want to affirm this dignity 'in spite of everything', in spite of all the contradicting evidence. In this 'in spite of everything' there is a seed of doubt, but it does not detract from the faith, which even seems to be strengthened by it. We will see that this 'in spite of everything' is a characteristic element of all theological virtues.

Hope

The 'in spite of everything' points to a paradox that is characteristic of the theological virtues. This is perhaps most clearly visible in hope. To see that, we must be aware that the kind of hope at stake here is an expectation that in fact goes against all expectations. The theological virtue of hope is not about the attitude of the person who estimates what is to come and, on that basis, 'has high hopes', that is to say: trusts that things will turn out well. Such a 'positive expectation' does not actually need 'the gift of hope'; it is based on experience and reasonable calculation, and perhaps on an optimistic disposition. However, the hope at stake here, hope as theological virtue, is an expectation that goes against reason. This hope always has the character of 'and yet'; it always goes 'against better judgement': although everything indicates that it is going downhill with the natural environment, or with a fair distribution of wealth, some people still manage to keep hope for a better future. This is not the same as the indifference of someone who thinks that everything will be fine, but rather the other way around: the utopia that makes people continue to commit themselves to what, all things considered, may seem hopeless.

That is why a pessimistic Greek perspective interpreted hope in a completely different way: according to this tradition, it was the worst of all the poisoned gifts with which Zeus punished humanity. Prometheus' theft of fire was punished through Pandora. From the box she received from the gods all possible ailments spread over the earth. Only hope remained. By this hope the other punishments (struggle, poverty, disease and mortality) were endlessly extended. Had we not had hope, we would soon put an end to this miserable life; but through hope – after all, if it were not for hope, the heart would break – we keep our feet, and we endure our misery.

Utopian thinking in this sense is non-Greek, but rather based on the (Jewish and) Christian interpretation of hope. It argues the other way round: in hope, the future always wins from the past. The burden of the past can become very heavy; 'what's done cannot be undone'; what has happened seems to determine what will happen. But the fact that we do not succumb to the burden of the past, we owe to hope. Through hope, what is negative in the present, what is wrong, what is imperfect, becomes a promise of fulfilment. It is clear that we cannot bring about this reversal of perspective, from hopeless despair to a hopeful future by ourselves. Even those who do not speak of 'God' will recognize that you can 'regain' hope or 'lose' all hope. This experience has been expressed by Christianity in the God-given virtue of hope.

Love

Just as the virtue of faith was something other than an uncertain opinion, and just as the virtue of hope is something other than a more or less reasonable expectation, so love as a theological virtue must also be distinguished from love as we understand it, either as a passionate force or as a reasonable devotion. Passion only needs an object to ignite. Passion is the ability to be attracted and the attractiveness of the object motivates and explains the love for it. The care parents have for their children is a form of love that involves passion as well as other aspects. The 'love' or care of doctors for their patients, and of teachers for their students, is yet another form of love. But these forms are also reasonable and can be explained from the kinship that exists or the task that one has. All this is different from the virtue that is at stake here: *caritas*.

What this love means is marked by the same paradox we already saw in faith and hope: this love loves precisely what cannot reasonably be called attractive, and this love devotes itself to people despite the fact that there are no ties of kinship or affection, and without an agreement or position that would oblige it. Perhaps the best way to illustrate this love is to use what in the Christian tradition is called 'the works of mercy'. There are seven corporal and seven spiritual works of mercy. The corporal works of mercy include, for example, visit the imprisoned, that is to say, looking for those whom we have justly – and usually with good reason – excluded. Caring for the sick was especially important for those who – understandably – nobody wanted to care for, because they were infectious and repulsive: the lepers. To shelter foreigners is not so much about taking in welcome guests, but those who disturb one's own peace; not about the people who have been granted a refugee status and towards whom we have a legal obligation, but rather about 'illegal immigrants' and all those who 'do not deserve' to be helped or housed. It seems that this love is blind, as they say. However, that is a misconception. Passionate love can be blind. But according to Christian tradition, charity sees more and sees more sharply than an ordinary person. It sees in the prisoner, the sick, the hungry, the thirsty, the stranger, the naked and the dead, Christ Himself.

Philosopher Paul Moyaert has shown, in the light of some of the works of mercy, that this is not about an action that can be called 'useful'. The dead no longer benefit from being buried, and 'praying' was once described by Moyaert as 'helping where helping no longer helps'. In his opinion, it is precisely this uselessness that points to the very nature of charity, to the radical nature of this form of love, and this explains why this virtue, too, does not arise from a natural desire, but must be given to us.

A secular form of this love can perhaps be found in gratitude. Not gratitude for a gift we receive from someone, but gratitude that you can sometimes feel for your existence and that is an aspect of the experience that life is good. Especially when that experience has something paradoxical, because at the same time you realize that much is not good at all, this virtue of love becomes visible. Perhaps the film *La vita è bella* gives a good example. Life is not just good, it is good 'in spite of everything'. You cannot have this experience through practice. Nevertheless, you can do a lot to achieve it. But in the end it happens to you – or it doesn't. It is, theologically speaking, a matter of grace.

4 Evaluation and continuation

Virtue ethics was profoundly Greek; it was translated, appropriated and adapted by Christianity, but as a result Christianity itself adapted to the Greek way of thinking. However, this adaptation does not alter the fact that the two roots of European culture remain distinct. Thus, although the theological virtues are worded in the (classical) language of virtues, it turns out that they use this language to say something radically new.

4.1 The two sides of theological virtues

With these theological virtues we have indeed struck upon a completely different path from that of classical virtue ethics. Anyone who loves, hopes and believes in the way of these virtues is probably no longer interested in the honour paid to him or her by his or her fellow citizens or in the recognition he or she receives for his or her generosity. In particular, the love of charity puts everything else into perspective. Augustine, who stood at the beginning of the history of the Christianization of virtues, is often quoted as saying *dilige et quod vis fac*: if you have love, you can do whatever you want.

The theological virtues clearly have two sides: on the one hand they are an important addition to the Greek virtues, on the other hand they are a dangerous one. They are important because they show a different moral quality from that which we already knew. This way they also prevent virtue from becoming bourgeois respectability. After all, these new virtues are so exorbitant that it is immediately clear that moral quality is different from 'obediently doing what is expected of you'. Moreover, they do justice to the experience that moral quality is not just a question of 'doing the best you can', however important that may be. Both in those who 'have it' and in those who miss it, there is – in addition to all their own merit – something that is not their own. The theological virtues thus warn against an exaggerated moral activism and remind us of the importance of a certain passivity. If living is an art, that art consists not only in doing what we can to become 'good', but also in developing the ability to receive what is given to us, or to endure what is withheld from us. Every artist will confirm that creating art is hard work, but at the same time you have to 'let it happen' as well.

On the other hand, this also poses a danger. Not only the danger of too much passivity (the Christian tradition has always produced *and* fought forms of quietism), but also the seemingly opposite danger of fanaticism. If virtue does not have its basis in my own activity and insight and if it is not guided by my own intelligence, then there seem to be no limits to what it asks of me. Not only will what I do never be enough (who has ever shown enough mercy?), but the limitations of reality will no longer play a role. The line between religious worship and dangerous madness, between the revolutionary hero and the ruthless wise guy, is in danger of fading. An artist must remain true to his or her inspiration, but not become blind to what his or her surroundings say and what his or her body demands. The same goes for the expert in the art of living well.

Whoever sees the two sides of the theological virtues will conclude that they should not be separated from the classical virtues. They put the Greek virtues in perspective, but the latter must protect the theological virtues against fanaticism and madness. This means that it is not easy to keep them together: they are a mutual criticism of each other. Moral life, too, is bound to be a tense affair. The next chapter will focus on an author who made 'tension' and 'struggle' the core of his thinking: Friedrich Nietzsche. Besides this fact, there is another, more important reason to reserve a place for him in a reflection on virtue ethics and the art of living well.

4.2 Virtues after the death of God

The Christian adaptation of virtue ethics shows that there is something in moral perfection we cannot (at least not entirely) choose and do by ourselves. With this, the Christian virtues show, even more sharply than the classical (Greek) virtues, a contrast between virtue ethics and the contemporary philosophy of the art of living well. These virtues show that the good is not simply an extension of the natural desire, and that in order to do good, it is not enough to simply 'know what we want', make a choice and have a little perseverance. However challenging this thought may be, that in our virtue we also depend on something other than our own efforts, it does contrast with the modern view of life that focuses on our own autonomy. I would therefore like to address in another way the question of whether this attention to virtues, and in particular their Christian interpretation, is not an anachronism.

For Christianity it was not a problem to speak of virtues as something we receive instead of acquire ourselves. It was already clear who would be the giver of these virtues: God. It is therefore no coincidence that attention to these virtues arises precisely in the context of Christianity. It is equally understandable that this attention is disappearing in a time and culture that is secularizing and from which the memory of Christianity is disappearing ever further. The same applies to the art of living well, as we saw in the previous chapter.

Can those Christian, theological virtues still have any real meaning for people who are not religious, in a time that seems to be thoroughly 'post-Christian', after 'the death of God'? I have given 'secular parallels' for the Christian virtues of faith, hope and love, but to what extent do they mirror a Christian culture that – at least in Europe – seems to be over? What is one to do with virtues that are 'received' in a time when there is no longer a 'giver'?

We must even face the possibility that speaking about virtues is altogether outdated, even without the presence of God and 'divine' virtues. In a time when metaphysics has been exchanged for science, the background of the classical Greek virtues seems to have been deprived of its self-evidence. Aristotle relied on a good order in nature, so that virtue could be understood in line with this nature (natural desire). Modern science, however, 'knows' that nature is in itself neither good nor evil. All that nature is, is matter that we can use to help shape what we know about what is good and evil, what we believe is right and wrong, and what it is that we desire and choose. Virtue ethics seems to belong to premodern thinking, whereas we (think we) have already passed beyond modernity and name ourselves 'postmodern'.

In the last two chapters I will be addressing these questions. Chapter VI focuses on this underlying view of the nature of man. First, in Chapter V, I will look at what Friedrich Nietzsche, an author from the beginning of our 'postmodern' times, has to say about virtue. Nietzsche is seen by both the art of living well and by many postmodern authors as a kind of patron of our new era. And indeed, he fights traditional metaphysics and Christianity more radically than most other thinkers. The 'death of God' he explicitly proclaimed is the beginning of a 'revaluation of all values', and it is therefore sure to deal with virtues once and for all. Or is it?

Literature

Aquinas, Thomas (ScG) (1974–96), *Summa contra Gentiles / Summe gegen die Heiden*, Darmstadt: Wissenschaftliche Buchgesellschaft [Latin–German].

Aquinas, Thomas (STh) (2006), *Summa Theologica*, Cambridge: Cambridge University Press.

Aristotle (EN) (1975), *Ethica Nicomachea*, trans. H. Rackham, Cambridge, MA/London: Loeb Classical Library.

Augustine (1998), *The City of God Against the Pagans (De civitate Dei)*, Cambridge: Cambridge University Press.

Augustine (2009), *Confessions (Confessiones)*, Oxford: Oxford University Press.

Becker, Marcel (1997), *Deugdethiek en pacifisme. Tolstojs pacifisme in gesprek met de deugdethiek van Aristoteles en Thomas van Aquino*, Amsterdam: Thesis Publishers.

Bernasconi, R. (1992), 'At War Within Oneself: Augustine's Phenomenology of the Will in the Confessions', in P. van Tongeren, P. Sars, C. Bremmers and K. Boey (eds), *Eros and Eris: Contributions to a Hermeneutical Phenomenology*, 57–66, Dordrecht: Kluwer.

Bovendeert, Jasmijn (2007), 'Kardinale deugden gekerstend. De vier kardinale deugden vanaf Ambrosius tot het jaar 1000', dissertation, Radboud Universiteit, Nijmegen.

Cicero, Marcus Tullius (1991), *On Duties (De Oficiis)*, Cambridge: Cambridge University Press.

Comte-Sponville, André (2002), *A Short Treatise on the Great Virtues*, London: Vintage.

Huysmans, J.-K. (1969), *Against the Grain (A rebours)*, trans. Havelock Ellis, New York: Dover Publishing Inc.

Moyaert, Paul (1998), *De mateloosheid van het christendom: Over naastenliefde, betekenisincarnatie en mystieke liefde*, Amsterdam: SUN.

Philips, Jos (2007), *Affluent in the Face of Poverty: On What Rich Individuals Like Us Should Do*, Amsterdam: Amsterdam University Press.

Pieper, J. (1998), *Das Viergespann: Klugheit, Gerechtigkeit, Tapferkeit, Maß*, Munich: Kösel.

Popov, Linda Kavelin (1997), *The Family Virtues Guide*, Ringwood, Vic.: Penguin.

Sarraute, Nathalie (2013), *Childhood*, trans. B. Wright, Chicago: University of Chicago Press.

Velde, R., te, ed. (1995), *De deugden van de mens: Thomas van Aquino: De virtutibus in communi*, Baarn: Ambo.

Tongeren, Paul van (2000), 'Die Tugenden des Besitzers', in Z. Frenyó, F.L. Lendvai, M.F. Fresco and P. van Tongeren (eds), *Orientations: Papers presented to the conferences of Dutch and Hungarian Philosophers 1986–1990*, 73–82, Maastricht: Shaker.

Tongeren, Paul van (2013), 'Natural Law, Human Dignity and Catholic Social Teaching', *Religion, State & Society*, 41(2): 152–63.

Tongeren, Paul van (2015), 'How Theological Are the Theological Virtues?' in Harm Goris, Lambert Hendriks and Henk Schoot (eds), *Faith, Hope and Love: Thomas Aquinas on Living by the Theological Virtues*, 45–60, Leuven: Peeters.

Vernant, J-P. (1981), 'Intimations of the Will in Greek Tragedy', in J.-P. Vernant and P. Vidal-Naquet (eds), *Myth and Tragedy in Ancient Greece*, trans. J. Lloyd, 28–62, Brighton: Harvester Press.

Patience

Sometimes it seems as if people are getting more and more impatient. Is it a problem if we lose our patience, that is to say: lose our ability to wait patiently? Can't we say that patience is a virtue of the past? In a time when the stagecoach was the fastest means of transport, you inevitably had to wait a long time for an answer after sending a letter. Patience helped. Patience was made a virtue out of necessity; but what would be lost if this virtue were to disappear because it is no longer needed? Thanks to the internet we can reach each other immediately and at any time, we are constantly 'connected'.

Unsurprisingly, waiting is difficult for us: every skill becomes stronger through practice and declines when it is no longer put into practice. So the less we have to wait, the less capable we will be of doing so. Does that matter if we have less need of it?

The curious thing is that patience does not just fade away or disappear as something that is no longer needed, but is replaced by impatience. The faster we can travel, communicate, produce, the more difficult it seems to be to endure the time it does take.

The speed with which we fly to distant destinations also increases the annoyance about waiting at airports. We send someone an email or text message and become impatient if we don't get an immediate response. We tap restlessly with our fingers on the desktop when it takes a minute or so before our computer has booted and we are 'finally' online.

There still seems to be enough reason to make it a virtue. But is patience a virtue? Virtues are perfections; what is perfected in patience? If we are impatient, we are bothered that we are not yet where we want to be, that we don't have the desired thing, or that the person we long for is not yet there. We only think of what we want to have; where we want to be and aren't at the moment. As far as we are in the 'here and now', we experience this only in negative terms: we are *not yet* allowed in, she is *not yet* there. In the time that separates us from what we want, there is nothing left but waiting.

If we cannot do what we want to do, we wait. How could 'waiting' itself be something we can 'do', something we can 'practise' in order to that we can become better at it? If this is possible, we should at least focus on that, and not just on what we can't do or don't have (yet). How do we do that: focus on waiting itself, and not just on what we are waiting for?

Once when I was waiting for the lift with a visiting colleague, I was annoyed because it took so long (again). I wanted to be on time at our next destination; and I was bothered by all those people using the lift on the first few floors of the building, while we were waiting sixteen floors up. When I apologized to my guest, not for my irritation, but for the waiting time, he was surprised. He was not annoyed at all. On the contrary: for him, these moments of waiting were the most beautiful moments of a day: 'All day we have to do all kinds of things, but now we don't need to do anything, because we can't do anything; this is really "free" time.'

We usually spend so much time with all possible activity that we are not really present. Only when our activity is interrupted – a lift that won't come, a traffic light that is red – can we have time, that is, have attention for time (unless, of course, we only think of the things we cannot do at that moment).

V NIETZSCHE AND/OR ARISTOTLE

At the end of Chapter III, I mentioned the 'two-and-a-half-thousand-year-long tradition' of virtue ethics: from approximately 500 BC to the present day. In Chapter IV we learned about the renewal that took place in European culture through Christianity and its significance for the tradition of virtue ethics. In this chapter we will focus on Nietzsche, who writes a 'Law against Christianity', 'Given on the Day of Salvation, on the first day of the year one (−30 September 1888, according to the false calculation of time)' (Nietzsche, AC, 254). He wants to start a new era! There is no clearer way to distance yourself from tradition. For good reason, it seems, Alasdair MacIntyre formulates his plea for a reorientation on virtues as a choice between 'Aristotle or Nietzsche' (1981: 103).

MacIntyre indeed develops his rehabilitation of virtue ethics in part through a critique of Nietzsche's thesis. According to him, Nietzsche is the 'emotivist' counterpart of Aristotelian virtue ethics. Nietzsche was the Kamehameha II of morality. This king of Hawaii (1797–1824) was said to have abolished any traditional taboos in his kingdom after they had in fact already lost their context. And Nietzsche had done the same with morality as such. After he had rightly determined (according to MacIntyre) that the modern project to find a rational foundation for morality had failed, he (wrongly) concluded that morality had abolished itself. What Nietzsche had not seen – again according to MacIntyre – was that this attempt at rational foundation was itself the result of the fact that since modernity (i.e. after the Middle Ages) philosophy had renounced Aristotle and his virtue ethics. That is why, according to MacIntyre, we should not go with Nietzsche and his dissolution of morality, but back to Aristotle, insofar as that is still possible.

Is MacIntyre right? Do we have a choice to make? Is it indeed the case that we either stick with virtues, inevitably making us premodern, or that we are modern and therefore inevitably have to let go of thinking in terms of virtues as well as perhaps any kind of moral language?

In this chapter we will see that this is a false choice. Nietzsche's thinking is not so much an alternative to, but rather a form of, virtue ethics. Just as we learned from Augustine and Aquinas how Greek virtue ethics developed through its reception in Christianity, so we can learn from Nietzsche how Greek–Christian virtue ethics can develop in a post-Christian and postmodern culture. The first development turned out to be one of translation and interpretation, differentiation and arrangement, and addition. What does the second development teach us?

1 The immoralist and virtue ethics

It may be surprising to see Nietzsche's thinking presented as a variant within virtue ethical tradition. Is this German thinker not the immoralist par excellence? Surely he is the one who criticizes morality and ethics more vehemently and radically than any other author. He brings moral prejudices to light and exposes moral hypocrisy. Ethical theories are revealed as preaching to the converted. And if there is any moral engagement in all this criticism, in all likelihood it does not concern what *we* tend to call 'moral' – which, after all, Nietzsche puts aside as 'slave morality' – but rather what he calls 'master morality'. And since the latter seems to be characterized by a culture of hardness and cruelty, by a deep awareness of human inequality and of the importance of keeping distance and hierarchy, even by a glorification of struggle and war, we are hardly able or willing to consider it as moral. Even apart from the absence of the specific characteristics of virtue ethics, it seems as if Nietzsche does not busy himself with any ethics at all, but only with an anti-ethics and a critique of ethics.

I don't intend to go into detail here about why there is indeed a certain morality in Nietzsche's critique of morality, which nevertheless doesn't detract from the comprehensiveness and radicalness of his critique. For an elaboration of this point, I refer to other publications, that are mentioned at the end of this chapter. Here I focus only on the question of how his thinking relates to virtue ethics. The broader context of Nietzsche's thinking about morality is partly presupposed, but where necessary it will be made explicit from this specific point of view.

It is hardly surprising that Nietzsche was at least well aware of the ancient virtue ethics. He was trained as a classical philologist and worked for ten years as a professor in that field in Basel. The great authors from the beginning of the virtue ethical tradition were therefore certainly not unknown to him. Plato was more important to him than Aristotle. During his years as a professor, he and his students read almost all of Plato's dialogues. When Nietzsche speaks of virtues we are often reminded of Plato: he mentions on several occasions four 'cardinal virtues' (which we do not find as such in Aristotle), and Platonic themes such as the unity of virtue and the importance of the good order of all faculties in a human being are easily recognizable. But Aristotle is certainly not absent. Nietzsche's ideal of 'nobility' is very similar to Aristotle's sketch of 'magnanimity' (*megalopsychia*). The importance of exercise and character formation in the virtue ethics of Aristotle is recognizable in Nietzsche's work as well. Apart from the views of Plato and Aristotle, the Hellenistic theories are discussed several times. He usually speaks very negatively about Stoicism, though he recognizes a lot in Epicurus. The importance of friendship is one of the many points in which Nietzsche has a strong affinity with this Hellenistic thinker.

Nietzsche, as a philologist or philosopher, never really studied authors from the Middle Ages, the period that is so important for the Christian interpretation and expansion of virtue ethics. However, this Christian interpretation was by no means unknown to him. As the son of a pastor, and surrounded by family members (from both his mother's and his father's side) who played a prominent role in the Lutheran church, he was brought up with Christianity. He certainly read the *Confessions* of Augustine, and Thomas Aquinas is quoted extensively in his *Genealogy of Morals*. Nietzsche probably hardly knew Aquinas first-hand, but through his lifelong friend, the church historian Franz Overbeck. He was also undoubtedly well informed by all the theological and historical literature he read. With the Christian author Pascal, Nietzsche had a similar love–hate relationship as he had with the character of Socrates. In his knowledge of and struggle with the Christian tradition, Christian virtues certainly play an important role, as we shall see.

The fact that Nietzsche was very sceptical about the merit of virtues, that he thought they were a way in which people tried to brush themselves up, to hide their true nature and in doing so ultimately spoiling that nature, certainly has to do with the state in which virtue ethics had ended up in the eighteenth century and in Nietzsche's own nineteenth century. It is the period in which this form of ethics became extremely petit bourgeois and – in the words of Max Scheler (1955: 15) – had degenerated into a 'quarrelsome, toothless old hag'. Nietzsche identifies virtue with stupidity and boredom, and compares faith in virtue with that venerable long pigtail of a concept which our grandfathers fastened to the backs of their heads, and often enough also to the backside of their understanding' (BGE, 214).

Because of the fierceness of his criticism, we risk overlooking the other side of his thinking. And with Nietzsche there is always another side. We can already suspect such a thing when we see that almost every attempt to rehabilitate virtue ethics, as we have seen it since the beginning of the twentieth century, always establishes a connection with Nietzsche. We already saw that MacIntyre did so by turning away from Nietzsche. However, every now and then, we also see another pattern. Max Scheler (1955) pleads for a rehabilitation of virtues through his elaboration on humility and respect: two virtues that are strongly shaped by Christianity, for which he nevertheless also seeks – and finds – support in Nietzsche. The same can be said of thinkers such as the British, Catholic, analytical philosopher Gertrud Anscombe on the one hand, and the German continental thinker Manfred Riedel on the other; their plea for a return to virtue ethics goes hand in hand with a great and positive interest in Nietzsche's thinking. Not so long ago the Australian philosopher Christine Swanton (2003) even published a book in which she develops a new, 'pluralistic' take on virtue ethics based on Nietzsche. According to her, we do not have to choose between either Nietzsche on one side or virtue ethics on the other, but rather Nietzsche can help to renew it. Not 'Nietzsche *or* Aristotle' (as MacIntyre suggests), but 'Nietzsche *and* Aristotle'. But first let's read Nietzsche himself.

2 Socratic, Christian and Nietzschean virtues

What did Nietzsche himself write about virtues, about classical or Greek, as well as Christian virtues and, perhaps, about new, Nietzschean virtues? His oeuvre is too multifaceted and the question is too extensive for one section. On the other hand, we must avoid being too far removed from his thinking by giving only a broad outline of it. That is why I will start from a small piece of text and try to explain it by using a wider range of texts from his work.

In Nietzsche's book *Daybreak* we find this aphorism:

A virtue in process of becoming. – Such assertions and promises as those of the antique philosophers concerning the unity of virtue and happiness or the Christian "But seek ye first the kingdom of God and his righteousness; and all these things shall be added unto you!" have never been made with total honesty and yet always without a bad conscience: one has advanced such propositions, which one very much desires to be true, boldly as the truth in the face of all appearance and has felt in doing so no religious or moral pang of conscience – for one had transcended reality *in honorem majorem* of virtue or of God and without any selfish motive! Many worthy people still stand at this *level of truthfulness*: when they feel themselves selfless, they think they are permitted to *trouble themselves* less about truth. Notice, however, that *honesty* is among neither the Socratic nor the Christian virtues: it is the youngest virtue, still very immature, still often misjudged and taken for something else, still hardly aware of itself – something in process of becoming which we can advance or obstruct as we think fit.

M, 456

It seems that Nietzsche distinguishes three kinds of virtues in this text, two of which we have already seen extensively: the Socratic (or Greek) and the Christian. To this he adds as a third kind of virtue, which seems to be characteristic of his own unmasking, desecrating, critical thinking: namely *honesty* or *truthfulness*. This suggests that in addition to the virtues of tradition, which Nietzsche criticizes, there is another virtue for those who have shaken off tradition. He seems to be speaking the language of self-confident Enlightenment thinkers, who believe that they are far ahead of their myth-linked predecessors. We will see, however, that it is not that simple: that honesty is not an obvious virtue, and that the Greek and even the Christian tradition are not unequivocally rejected. As I have already said, there is always another side to Nietzsche's thought.

2.1 Honesty

The seventh chapter of *Beyond Good and Evil*, entitled 'Our virtues', focuses on honesty or truthfulness. Nietzsche often refers to this virtue as 'the youngest among the virtues'. Anyone who reads these texts carefully will see that there is always a hesitation in them and that it is not clear to what extent Nietzsche attributes this virtue to himself.

On the one hand, this honesty is indeed the core of Nietzsche's morality. It is only because of fearless honesty that he dares to look beyond the masquerades of morality and religion and pierce them. Who dares to acknowledge – to name but a few of the examples that Nietzsche's texts are full of – that self-sacrifice is a subtle form of selfishness, that the martyr enjoys the sense of power he or she shows and acquires, that every friendship would be broken if the friends knew everything about each other, that man and woman seek in love respectively domination and submission or devotion, and so on? Who dares to acknowledge this in such a way, that he or she actually applies it to himself? In order to commit, as it were – again, an image of Nietzsche – vivisection on yourself, one does indeed need such a genuine honesty. Honesty is the virtue of the radical critic.

This genuine honesty will not spare itself either. It will discover that in that honesty a cruelty persists, that enjoys the pain that the thinker inflicts on him- or herself. In this cruelty it will recognize the law that applies to all living things, which Nietzsche calls the 'will to power'. And... it will discover that it is not so much a moral quality as some sort of instinct that people obey. With this, however, the investigation loses its (moral) sanctioning and raises the question as to why it is carried out with such zeal. Or to put it another way: if the suspicious critic discovers that 'truth' is a construction motivated by a rudimentary pursuit of self-preservation or the expansion of power – what is the truth of this discovery itself worth? That which motivates the investigation becomes the object of investigation itself, or in a metaphor of Nietzsche: 'the element required to heat the machine seems to be the same element as is to be investigated by means of the machine.' (cf. HAH II.2 WS, 43).

What does that mean for honesty as virtue? That it is not just 'the youngest among the virtues', but – as Nietzsche indeed calls it – it is also 'the last virtue'. 'Who enters this labyrinth must be prepared to lose the way' (cf. BGE, 214). 'We sail right over morality, we crush, we destroy perhaps the remains of our own morality by daring to make our voyage there' (cf. BGE, 23). The radical questioner will regard also his own questions 'as questionable' (HAH II.2 WS § 43) – these are all paraphrases of texts that can be found in abundance in Nietzsche's work. This means that the virtue of honesty may well start the criticism, but that it does not survive the process itself. Those who speak with moral superiority about their own radical criticism are naive: they pretend that the criticized morality can still add value to its criticism. It is the same naivety that we see in reductionist theories about man. Scientists (or more often: scientific journalists and people who read their texts) suggest that many of the ideas we have about ourselves are illusions and that we are in fact 'no more than' … you name it: animals, genes, brain processes. Rarely, however, is this discovery applied to the self-awareness that shows itself in the importance that people attach to that knowledge. Book titles such as 'We Are Our Brain' or 'Free Will Does Not Exist' show a lack of self-criticism. Those who think they can leave the old morality behind them and stand firmly on their own moral soil do not know what they are dealing with. It is more likely that in real life this person (for example, if he or she 'chooses' to unmask free will as an illusion, or if he or she considers it 'important' to convey this message about the brain) secretly, and thus untruthfully, parasitizes all those things that were denounced as illusions in his criticism.

Nietzsche cannot be accused of such naivety and untruthfulness. Not because he holds himself back in his critical unmasking – on the contrary! – but because he always applies this criticism to himself. His thinking and his life constantly show the effects of this: radical displacement, profound doubt and despair, distressing loneliness. Nietzsche does not secretly cling to the morality he criticizes, but experiments with a radical immoralism that inevitably frightens anyone who reads him accurately. In this experiment, he is not only the experimenter who remains out of shot himself, but he himself becomes a battlefield in which 'self-sufficiency and truthfulness fight each other' (cf. GS, 110).

With this we seem further removed than ever from Nietzschean ethics, let alone virtue ethics. Is MacIntyre right with his dilemma: we either go back to Aristotle if we still want liveable ethics, or go on into the desert with Nietzsche? I don't think so. I think Nietzsche's work shows that the desert is also a fallow land, where anything can grow up, even new forms of the old virtues. For although his own virtue, honesty, is not a refuge from criticism, criticism is not the destruction of that which is exposed. We will see that this applies to his criticism of both Greek and even Christian virtues. The combination of criticism of and commitment to virtues is an example of what he himself calls 'revaluation': a transformative reinterpretation.

2.2 Temperance

In the quotation I used as a starting point, Nietzsche spoke of the 'Socratic virtues'. This expression refers to the Greek virtues, as we find them not only in Aristotle, but also in Plato's texts on Socrates. Nietzsche refers in particular to the four virtues that were later called 'cardinal virtues', but which also appear in Plato as the four core virtues: courage, temperance, prudence and justice.

Without a doubt, the Socratic virtues in general and each of these four cardinal virtues are all subject to Nietzsche's criticism. According to him, the Greek virtues all suffer from an overestimation of reason and from the demonstrably false superstition that being virtuous would somehow make us happy. Nietzsche criticizes justice as a virtue that does not recognize the natural order (and thus inequality) between people, and prudence as an instrument by which physically weaker people tried to get rid of their masters. He seems to reframe courage as something needed in the fight against morality, and temperance to him is an emergency measure for people who cannot control themselves.

However, we also find all four of them in a positive context. The criticism of justice presupposes that we can 'do justice' to natural differences and their conflicting interests. Nietzsche's writings are an exercise in self-knowledge, which is the core of moral reasoning. Courage or bravery is a core virtue of the dangerous experimentation in which his criticism exists. And even the virtue of temperance reappears in a positive sense, as we will see. I will only elaborate Nietzsche's criticism, especially its downside, with regard to this last virtue.

Nietzsche criticizes the virtue of temperance when, or as far as, it is aimed at eradicating passions and thus betrays contempt for physical life. According to Nietzsche, only a person who is too weak to shape those passions can have such contempt. However, this criticism clearly hides a positive understanding of the virtue of temperance, for to 'shape' these passions is to temper them. Nietzsche indeed criticizes the lack of moderation in the obsession for collecting things of his time and culture; in Christianity's demand of absolute devotion; in ascetic morality and in its smothering of our passions; and so on. Nietzsche's alternative, therefore, instead of being the opposite of temperance, would rather be the opposite of this excessiveness.

With this, classical philologist Nietzsche seems to fall back on one of the meanings of the Greek name for this virtue: *sophrosyne*. It does not stand for an extinction of forces, but for proportionality, that is to say: the balance of forces. This reveals a completely different dynamic than that of limitation, reduction, weakening, which was often associated with the virtue of temperance. Nietzsche somewhere compares it to the skill of a horseman – a comparison with a long tradition: Plato already used it and in the iconographic tradition the virtue of temperance is often depicted with a horse's bit and bridle. A good rider has to tame his horse, but that doesn't mean he or she has to take away all the wild forces! On the contrary, the rider must cultivate that wildness, master it and know how to use it for his or her own purposes. The more strength remains in the horse, the greater the challenge for the horseman, the more skilful his own riding. Weak horsemen can only master powerless horses. Therefore, for the weak, temperance will have to consist in eradicating or at least suppressing vital forces. The metaphor of horse and horseman makes it clear that real virtuosity or excellence (and that is the meaning of 'virtue', *virtus*, *arete*) can only be achieved by those who are strong enough to counterbalance strong forces, without having to destroy or weaken them. As with good riding, virtue will not only consist in controlling these forces, but also and above all in using them. The strengths of the horse and those of the horseman should, as it were, temper each other. This mutual temperance is precisely the meaning of the Greek virtue that Nietzsche brings to the fore.

Nietzsche's critique does not lead to a denial or neglect of the virtue of temperance, but to a reinterpretation of it. This reinterpretation gives the term a new meaning. In contrast to the bourgeois virtue of temperance, by which the weak acquired moral high ground, Nietzsche puts 'the pleasure of maintaining measure' (Unpublished Note, KSA 11.123, 25[420]): a challenging, dangerous virtue.

2.3 Faith, hope and love

Surprisingly as it may be, even the Christian virtues are not solely and unambiguously criticized by Nietzsche (though criticize them he certainly does). According to Nietzsche, Christianity is the religion of the weak, who, through a moral interpretation of their weakness, try to place themselves above the strong. The Christian virtues of faith, hope and love are the pinnacle of this false revaluation: they justify the resentment and hatred felt against strong people and they enable a continuation of hopeless suffering, by having faith in another world and thereby denying the reality in which one actually lives.

Nevertheless, Nietzsche is fascinated by these Christian virtues. He lucidly sees how they go against the rationality that is so central to the Greek virtues. According to Nietzsche, this rationality determined the weakness of the Greek virtues. These virtues were an attempt by the weak to tame, through reason, the instinctive powers of the strong. They tried to outwit the strong and take away their happiness and success, by promising a true happiness that was only visible and achievable through reason. Well, Christianity is a protest against this supremacy of reason. Christian virtues are completely unreasonable. They replace knowledge with faith, real assessments of opportunities and dangers with hope, and plain logic with love – which is, according to Nietzsche, 'the state in which man sees things most of all as they are *not*' (AC, 23).

The fact that Nietzsche was fascinated by these Christian virtues is not *despite*, but *because of* their unreasonableness. He criticizes the reasonableness of the Greek concept of virtue because, according to him, this Greek rationality was a kind of thinking focused on usefulness. Socrates tried to show that it was more sensible, that is: more profitable, more useful, to be virtuous. The Christian virtues do not seem interested in this kind of usefulness; they even explicitly seek the opposite. According to Nietzsche, they are a revolution against reason's domination of the affects, as pursued by Greek philosophy (cf. D, 58). Since Christianity was a plebeian religion, it may only have been the affects of the weak that were liberated, but the principle itself of resistance against the tyranny of rationality and utility remains valuable.

There is probably more to the Christian virtues that interests Nietzsche. As a philosopher of will, he is interested in these virtues which, as we saw (in Chapter IV.3.2), are virtues of will. Even the strangest aspect of these virtues – namely that they were not acquired by practice, but given by grace – will have fascinated Nietzsche, who was also an artist for whom inspiration played a major role. The fact that these virtues are given also creates a difference between people, which, although not completely absent in Greek virtue ethics, is much less prominent. In classical virtue ethics there are differences between exemplary and highly accomplished people on the one hand and the inexperienced or novices on the other, but it still suggests that in the end everyone can live virtuously, as long as he or she practises and tries his or her best. We saw (in Chapter III.3) how the philosophers of the art of living well adopted this element – which Nietzsche calls a 'democratic prejudice'. The Christian interpretation shows a different image. Not only do medieval theologians distinguish between virtues for everyone and virtues belonging to a certain group or state of life (monks for instance practise a different and much stricter way of life than lay people). But above all, the dependence on grace makes Christian virtues something for the 'chosen'. And although Nietzsche does not want to have anything to do with divine grace, he has an eye for strong individuals and realizes that their chosen status is at least to a large extent not by their own merit (cf. BGE, 274).

It is therefore not only as a parody that the Christian or theological virtues, faith, hope and love occasionally appear in Nietzsche in a positive sense. Against all threats of further 'mediocrity', 'worship' and 'diminution' of man, as he perceives them in Europe as a result of the prevailing morality of the weak, he still shows a hope and a belief in future healing. This faith and hope may be directed at humans and not at God, but they go against reasonable expectations as much as the Christian virtues did. Nietzsche even seems to beg for it, though his prayer is not directed at God, but at divine goddesses in the realm beyond good and evil assuming they exist' (GM, I.12).

In addition to 'faith' and 'hope', love – continuously mentioned as the most important in the Christian tradition, often in the words of St. Paul (1 Cor. 13.13) – is to Nietzsche, too, a virtue. Once again, of course, it cannot be found in Nietzsche's work in the Christian form of love as charity. He is interested in the love for one's (own) life. Even now, however, this is a kind of love that is by no means self-evident, but one that goes against all expectations and even against a certain aversion. 'It is the love for a woman that causes doubt in us.' (GS, preface 3). Somewhere he himself explicitly relates it to what, in his opinion, is 'the core of Christianity' (Unpublished Note KSA 8.180, 9[1]). More frequently we find love in the form of an embrace of fate (*amor fati*) or gratitude for life (cf. GS, 276) or for a thought that comes to him 'as a great liberator' (cf. GS, 324).

3 Nietzschean virtue ethics

With Nietzsche there is – as I said – always another side. He even incorporates aspects of the Christian virtues into his own thinking. What does this mean for us and our attempt to rethink classical virtue ethics for our own time? And what does it mean for the kind of realistic life questions that virtue ethics deals with, questions that I have raised in earlier chapters? What does it mean for the art of living well and for life as a work of art?

I do not mean to answer these and similar questions in terms of a Nietzschean ethics or doctrine of life. Such answers tend to forget that there is 'always another side' to Nietzsche's thinking; or they simply try to separate the 'wrong' Nietzsche from the 'right' Nietzsche. Perhaps we could find another way to take on the 'challenge' – as Christine Swanton (2003: 252) calls it – that Nietzsche poses to virtue ethics. This challenge consists in continuing to speak the same language of virtue ethics, but under completely different conditions from those of Aristotle. Swanton (1998) summarizes these other conditions as follows: according to Nietzsche (a) illness is the normal state of humans, (b) the successful persons seem to be sad figures, (c) most people are not suited to the real virtues, and (d) the world is imperfect. For her, this challenge leads to the development of an expressivist and pluralistic virtuosity, which is indeed inspired by Nietzsche, but which does not claim to be a Nietzschean form of ethics. Instead of deriving a concept of happiness or *eudaimonia* from a teleological concept of (human) nature and understanding virtue as that which leads to this happiness, she interprets virtue as the expression of a powerful and healthy life. The primary element of such a life is a healthy form of self-love: an affirmation of one's own life that is free from resentment and self-contempt, and that does not depend on the opinions of others or on external norms. Since people are different and also have different strengths, there are different kinds of virtues. They resemble each other in that they always bear witness to that healthy self-love and prevent mediocrity and decadence.

In the last section of this chapter, I would like to draw some other lines myself. In doing so, my ambitions are more modest than those of Swanton. I will not develop any new form of ethics, but will only try to indicate a few points as to how Nietzsche's way of speaking about virtues may help us in our task of shaping contemporary virtue ethic. What can Nietzsche teach us about what is and what is not essential for virtue ethics, about possibilities and difficulties for virtue ethics in our time? In answer to that question, I distinguish three elements: some aspects of virtue ethics are maintained even in the changed circumstances, some others need to be supplemented or reinterpreted, and others are a problem, albeit in a hopeful way.

3.1 What remains

The radical nature of Nietzsche's criticism, and the completely different presuppositions of his thinking compared to that of Aristotle, make the things that remain unchanged all the more striking and important. It would seem that these are characteristics of virtue ethics that are not attached to a particular and limited context.

We already saw this with regard to cardinal and even Christian virtues. Although their interpretation does not remain the same, these virtues apparently contain characteristics that cannot be attributed to one specific interpretation. Nietzsche's criticism of the Greek cardinal virtues can be summed up as follows: they are the needs of weak people, who have rationalized their lack of strength and self-confidence into a clever solution by which they want to protect themselves against other people and against their own passions. There is a challenge in this critique: to show that there are in fact 'strong' forms of courage, temperance, prudence and justice. With regard to the virtue of temperance, we have seen what that could mean. This virtue of measure does not consist in a reduction or weakening of one's own nature, but in the way in which you shape as many forces as possible – forces as strong as possible – within yourself. Nietzsche also calls this: 'giving style to one's character' (FW, 290). Virtue ethics after Nietzsche should, similarly, also learn to distinguish strong forms of other virtues from their forms that seem more like petit-bourgeois goodness.

In his criticism of the Christian virtues, Nietzsche, while rejecting the content of the Christian three, remains fascinated by the same virtues insofar as they are not the result of practice, but are somehow received, and thus given. In order to receive a gift, one must be receptive. This draws attention to the moral significance of a certain receptivity or passivity. In a recent book, two American authors, Dreyfus and Kelly, point out that this was also the core of the pre-Aristotelian, Homeric concept of virtue: in the world of Homer, virtue or excellence was fundamentally determined by a sense of gratitude, awe and wonder. They point out that the Greek word for virtue (*arete*) is etymologically related to the verb *araomai* meaning 'to pray'. Homer, according to them, knew that human excellence requires that you have a sense of what is 'holy' or 'awe-inspiring' and that you relate to it in an appropriate way (Dreyfus and Kelly 2011: 61). They also believe – and I think wrongly – that Nietzsche, although he knew Homer, overlooked this crucial aspect.

The most important characteristic of virtue ethics that endures Nietzsche's criticism is something else still. It concerns that which makes this form of ethics different from all other modern forms of ethics. In fact, it is only since the beginning of modern times that new forms of ethics have emerged, which from the seventeenth century onwards crystallized into new theoretical paradigms, with thinkers like Thomas Hobbes (1588–1679), Immanuel Kant (1724–1804) and Jeremy Bentham

(1748–1832). We can characterize them as respectively: contractualist ethics with which we solve problems concerning cooperation; deontological ethics, which concentrate on the duty that precedes every goal and every intention; and utilitarian ethics which concentrate on the effectiveness of how we achieve what we strive for (cf. Chapter II.2). And, of course, there are all kinds of hybrid forms of these three basic types. Typical of all three is, first, that they indicate how people should act and how actions can be judged and, second, that the consequences of action for other people are the most important criterion.

If we look at premodern virtue ethics and its postmodern form in Nietzsche's work against this modern background, we see that it is not about the action, but about the person. Moral quality does not primarily belong to what someone does at a certain moment, but rather to one's life as a whole, to the person whose life it is about and to the characteristics that make him or her who he or she is. Virtues are characteristics of a person who lives virtuously. Of course we recognize that quality in what we see of that person, but that is more than just his actions. The *way in which* someone acts (and does not act) is at least as important as *what* he or she does; and what someone does follows from who he or she is. Moreover, the focus is not so much on an assessment, let alone an assessment by others. Virtue ethics is about happiness and flourishing and therefore rather about the appreciation one has for oneself. In this, others and the community in which one lives play an important role, but not a defining one.

This way of thinking is by no means self-evident to us; it requires explanation in a time dominated by other moral concepts. The moral value referred to in virtue ethics can perhaps best be compared with the quality of an artist. We do not appreciate a great artist merely for each of his or her achievements. The artist's significance does not become greater or smaller because another work is attributed to his or her oeuvre, or because a work that was attributed to him or her turns out to be by someone else. We appreciate Vermeer – with his (supposed) mere forty-five paintings in total (thirty-three of which are preserved) – no less than Rembrandt, who made a hundred painted and twenty etched self-portraits alone, in addition to his many hundreds of other paintings and etchings and thousands of drawings. The genius of the great painter is evident in *each* of his or her works and is what makes the person behind these artworks so fascinating to us. And no matter how important recognition from others is in the life of an artist, ultimately even that importance also depends on the value he or she attributes to him- or herself, the extent to which he or she realizes his or her destiny.

From this perspective, it is all about the person and about life as a whole. The current dominance of primarily or exclusively action-oriented ethics often makes it difficult to keep sight of this. All too easily, virtue ethics is also involved in a structure of questions derived from these other forms of ethics. However, virtue ethics is not so much distinguished from other forms of ethics in that it provides a different *answer* to the same question ('what should I do?'), but in that it poses a different *question*, namely: 'how should I live?', 'what kind of a human being should I be?' And even this 'should I be' is still distorting: after all, this is not so much an obligation, let alone an obligation that would go against my natural inclination. Virtue ethics is about how someone realizes his destiny. That was not only true for Aristotle. Nietzsche shows that it is still the case. For both, that destiny was not imposed or offered by any God or other authority, but discovered in the praxis of life itself. Aristotle points out the importance of community and education, in which you learn what is worthwhile; Nietzsche calls it the task of the teacher to help the student discover what his destination is (cf. SE).

This realizing of your destiny happens (if it happens, or better: to the extent in which it happens) in a life as a whole. Of course that life takes place in all kinds of choices and actions. And others are always involved. Some actions are more decisive for the person we become than others; some have more effects on other people than others. Whoever breaks a 'promise for life' does something to life as a whole; and not just his own, but also for that of the person to whom the promise is made. All choices and actions remain part of that life as a whole, which is never finished as long as one lives, so that the meaning of those actions and choices can never be definitive. They continue to acquire their meaning from someone's life as it develops within a community.

Although what has been done cannot be undone, its meaning is not fixed in the interpretation of one person, at one moment. Nevertheless, there is something permanent in this constant changeability. That lasting thing, your own life, also has a style, which gives it a sense of unity. Moreover, that life is not an abstract subject that always remains the same; it is an evolving course of life. A person's life course and lifestyle are important points of attention for virtue ethics.

3.2 What changes

In the preceding section I wrote that it is primarily about self-esteem. Nietzsche characterizes the noble soul – his version of what Aristotle calls the virtuous man – by his 'reverence for himself' (BGE, 287). As I said before, the community plays an important, but not all-determining role in this. Presumably, at this point something has changed between Aristotle and Nietzsche, between antiquity and our time.

For Aristotle, the (political) community was the self-evident context within which a virtuous life was possible. According to him, no human life is possible at all outside this community, let alone a good, successful, happy life. In his *Politics* he writes that the one who lives outside the political community is either less than a human being or more than a human being, that is to say: either an animal or a god (cf. Chapter I.5). Nietzsche seems to allude to this when he writes in his *Twilight of Idols*: 'To live alone one must be an animal or a god – says Aristotle. There is yet a third case: one must be both – a *philosopher...*' (TI, *Maxims and Arrows*, 3). If we may assume that 'the philosopher' in this case stands for the kind of life Nietzsche considers as the ideal life, it is clear that for him the relationship between a happy person and the community is different than it was for Aristotle.

Nietzsche's aphorisms can never be explained in a single way. Even this short text contains several meanings. The main issue is that Nietzsche here seems to adopt Aristotle's suggestion that gods and (at least some) animals are solitary beings, but Nietzsche reverses the conclusion. While for Aristotle the only humane way of life is a life in community, and thus contrary to the life of an animal or a god, Nietzsche seems to refer to the highest form of life as a combination of animal and god, that is: as extremely solitary. The reason for this has to do with another line, along which Nietzsche, at second instance, criticizes Aristotle's suggestion about the solitary nature of gods and animals. For gods it may be true that they do not need each other (although they too, as long as they are with many, seem to be constantly working together), but with animals Nietzsche himself thinks first and foremost of herd animals. He does not take into account the way in which Aristotle precisely distinguishes between the kind of community that is the herd, and the human community, which rather takes the form of a conversation about interpretations (see Chapter I.7). According to Nietzsche, people usually live as herd animals. We already saw that his criticism of (virtue) ethics had precisely to do with this: virtues are the foundation of a morality with which the weak hold each other together to protect against the strong. In order to live not as an animal, but really as a human being, you have to detach yourself from the herd and become a solitary animal.

For Nietzsche, this requirement to be able to stand alone is linked to the exceptional task of the philosopher or the free spirit. In fact, in doing so he brings forward something that seems characteristic of the modern age: while premodern people were first and foremost members of a community (and from there they could become individuals), we are first and foremost individuals. Admittedly, we then do join in all kinds of forms of community, but without ever wanting to derive our identity entirely from it. We like to see ourselves as individuals who may form a community by making agreements and who may choose to become a member of a community, but never without an exit option; and for ourselves we never coincide with our membership of any community.

This is problematic for virtue ethics, which is not possible without community. People do not live alone, but are always interconnected with others in all kinds of ways, so that they cannot flourish without the success of others. The examples we imitate exist only within a moral community. Furthermore, recognition by others is an essential part of the complacency that comes with a successful life. How could a life succeed if it separated itself from that community? For Aristotle, this community is ultimately a political community, which according to him is *autark*, in other words, self-sufficient: it does not need anything outside of itself. Such a community is homogeneous enough to guarantee a stable moral consensus and heterogeneous enough to keep that consensus alive (see Chapter I.7). For us, such a community no longer exists. It is not easy to determine what our political community is: local, regional, national, European, global? Moreover, no political community, not even the local one, is a single entity, but rather a structure whose main purpose is to prevent the inevitable conflict between different beliefs and shape and limit interests. Modern political thinking, as has been said, starts with the individual and never frees itself from that. Our individualism poses a serious problem for virtue ethics. Nietzsche recognizes that problem.

As a result, he distinguishes two types of community. In contrast to the community he criticized – which, according to him, always somehow brings us down ('All community makes men – somehow, somewhere, sometime "common"'; BGE, 284) – Nietzsche proposes a different kind of community, one that is not given beforehand, but that is sought and desired: the community of the free spirits. The model for this utopian form of community is friendship. Instead of the public community of citizens, he places the intimate community of friends. Friendship – perhaps even more so than in the situation of Aristotle, for whom it was also a condition for a happy life – is vital for contemporary virtue ethics.

The relationship between individual and community is therefore subject to change, which does not diminish the role of that community, but does make it different and more difficult. Something similar is true for the relationship between body and soul and for the role of the soul. Classical virtue ethics is all about 'care for the soul'. The influence of Christianity in European culture has only increased the significance of the soul. Nowadays all emphasis seems to be on the body. Even that which used to be called the soul is now reduced to the body. Psychology, the science of the soul (*psychè*), wants to be 'real science' and therefore prefers to focus on what can be measured empirically. What we cannot perceive as brain function is folk psychology or epiphenomenon. For many people physical exercise and the gym have replaced the 'spiritual exercises' and the 'care for the soul' that was crucial for the ancient art of living (cf. Chapter III.2.1). Nietzsche seems to fit in with this development, if not having in part caused it through his criticism of Christianity and metaphysics. He emphasizes the role of the body and likes to characterize his own thinking as 'physio-psychology'.

Nietzsche does indeed criticize 'soul superstition' (cf. BGE, preface), but that is not the belief that humans have a soul, but the theory that attributes characteristics to the soul that it does not have, and that does not do justice to what it is. According to Nietzsche the soul is not eternal and immortal; it arises and grows during our life and is mortal like the body (cf. D, 501); according to Zarathustra, the soul even dies earlier than the body (cf. Z, prologue, 6). However, the denial of the immortality of the soul does not mean that the soul itself is also denied. Nietzsche even makes the soul the distinguishing characteristic of the human being. He states that the soul is the product of a development in which humans as such first came into being. After all, humans have gradually distinguished themselves from the animal by gaining depth, by acquiring an inner being – with which they not only became the most interesting among animals, but also susceptible to all kinds of new diseases (cf. GM, II 16).

What comes about phylogenetically in a long history must also come about again ontogenetically in the history of each individual human being: the soul is the whole and the result of the inner experiences of a human being (cf. BGE, 45). The soul expresses who and what someone is. Hence the previously discussed central place for the person instead of the action. Here again, the community plays a role. For in the history in which the experiences of (and to) a human being are collected, the fate of previous generations also has an impact (cf. BGE, 264). Therefore the soul cannot be one indivisible whole. On the contrary, it has many forms, or in other words: a person has not only one soul but consists of a whole organization of souls (cf. BGE, 19). This soul is also the core of humankind in Nietzsche's anthropology. He therefore criticizes the scientists who think that everything can be reduced to that which can be measured and recorded: the naturalists who 'as soon as they touch the soul, lose it too' (BGE, 12).

The soul reflects the body (cf. Z, preface, 3), but that in no way means that it is merely an epiphenomenon of the body; body and soul act upon each other. Nietzsche emphasizes that soul and body cannot be separated from each other (cf. GS, preface, 3), but that does not mean that they should not be distinguished. In love, for example, we desire not only the body of the loved one, but also his or her soul. After all, the lover wants the loved one to want him or her, that is to say, that he or she 'dwells in his or her soul' and perhaps even possesses it (cf. GS, 14). The health of the body is determined by the nature and condition of the soul (cf. GS, 120). Soul and body are one whole, but according to Nietzsche this unity of soul and body is not an identity but an interconnectedness. And this interconnectedness has many forms.

So the soul has by no means disappeared, but it is understood differently. This means that a form of virtue ethics under modern, Nietzschean conditions will still be a shaping of the soul, but not exactly the same soul as before. It will have to recognize that souls are different and that some things are only possible for certain souls. Moreover, the same things (books, films, experiences) can have very different meanings for different souls. Therefore, there is not one single virtue for all souls. On the contrary: as different as the souls are, so different will their healthy forms look (cf. GS, 120).

Moreover, we have already seen that souls themselves are multiple. People unite several souls within them, even more than the two that Goethe's Faust felt in him (cf. BGE, 244). This diversity of souls is not a neutral 'next to each other', but a hierarchy. After all, the soul stands for passion, for experiences of what matters. Only a soulless contemplation could therefore 'indifferently' place different souls side by side. For

Nietzsche it is clear that there is a ranking of souls, just as the soul itself is a ranking (cf. BGE, 263).

The health of the soul then has to do with the extent to which it can cope with its own multiplicity: that is to say, whether it is able to assemble and order that multiplicity or not. According to Nietzsche, the illness of today's culture consists, among other things, in the fact that the modern soul can no longer do this, that it is a chaos (cf. BGE, 224). The well-being of the soul requires organization and control of that multitude, but not at the expense of diversity, not even of the tensions between the different souls that a person assembles within him- or herself. According to Nietzsche it is about making this tension productive: only in this way can a person constantly overcome him- or herself (cf. BGE, 257), that is, distinguish him- or herself from the animal that has a fixed identity.

This requires a continuous exercise (cf. D, 42) and a continuous self-examination. And in this we recognize once more the tradition of virtue ethics. More than in its classical form, it will now pay attention to diversity: different people develop different virtues – the greater a person, the more possibilities he or she collects in him- or herself. We have already seen that the virtue of temperance derives its meaning precisely from this, which again confirms that there is a strong continuity between premodern and postmodern virtue ethics, despite and underneath all their differences.

3.3 Problems

Nevertheless: despite all the points of similarity and continuity between the positions that we summarize in the names of Aristotle and Nietzsche, there are indeed serious problems and challenges for a form of virtue ethics under contemporary conditions. The most fundamental of these have to do with the fact that a number of factual and fundamental presuppositions of Aristotelian ethics are contested in contemporary science and philosophy. I will briefly mention two, both of which can be linked to Nietzsche's thinking.

Aristotle assumes that attitudes (and as we know virtues are also attitudes) are not only created through actions, but are themselves the basis from which actions originate: you become a brave person by taking brave actions, and whoever is brave will act bravely in situations that occur. This is the structure of traditional education: we let our children act in a certain way, so that in the long run they will act in this way by themselves and on their own. Some contemporary human scientists dispute the correctness of this assumption: they show through experiments that people do not act so much on the basis of traits or beliefs, but that their actions are determined by the situation or by elementary survival instincts or other instincts. And situations and instincts are not the object of education.

Nietzsche asks one of the questions that arises from this in a very radical and provocative way: shouldn't we put biological terms like 'taming' and 'breeding' in the place of the idealistic and humanistic concept of 'education'? A few years ago the German philosopher Peter Sloterdijk repeated this possibility in a notorious speech published under the title 'Rules for the Human Zoo', in which he links Nietzsche's question to the anthropogenetic possibilities of modern science and technology. The now fashionable brain sciences give their own version of this possibility. I will not go into this here. In part this is once again a confusion of philosophy, as the way in which the subject interprets itself, and science, as the non-subject-bound explanation of factual processes. For that matter, I refer to what has been said about hermeneutics in Chapter II.

The criticism is really challenging only insofar as it is itself hermeneutical, i.e. proposing an alternative explanation. To this end, I will briefly formulate a second criticism, on which I will elaborate in the next chapter. The criticism relates to the optimistic teleological presupposition that underpins Aristotelian ethics. After all, it assumes that nature as a whole, as well as human nature, is 'well constructed'. That is why education can be compared to the work of a gardener. By pruning and caring, we help nature, which is already good in itself, to reach its flourishing. Thus the virtues are the optimal forms that the human intellect and human desire can take. In itself, the intellect wants nothing but insight and knowledge: after all, you can't desire to go astray! And as passionate beings, we have always been focused on what is good for us: self-preservation, protection against danger, and all kinds of social matters. Virtues are only the optimal forms that this natural desire can acquire through upbringing in a good community. This best possible form is one in which reason is leading, but this rationality is in fact already in nature itself. Our intellect only turns on the light, as it were, and in this way ensures that we see more clearly what we are already focused on.

This interpretation of nature and of ourselves is challenged by Nietzsche when he interprets nature as a will to power. Exploitation, domination, oppression, appropriation and so on are not unnatural excesses, but characterize precisely the essence of all life (cf. BGE, 259). This is no longer the nature that is *kosmos* and well constructed; rather, it resembles an exaggeration of the modern concept of nature, as we see it both in religion since the Reformation and in science since modernity: nature as a force that is fundamentally dangerous and threatening and that therefore has to be controlled, contained and submitted to us. And that is the language of modern ethics: norms and laws must limit the selfish nature of humankind. How would a form of virtue ethics – one 'in line with natural desire' – be compatible with such an understanding of nature? In the next chapter I would like to address this question using yet another formulation of this challenge. On the basis of what we have found in this chapter in Nietzsche's work, we can in any case conclude that he does know how to combine such a concept of nature with a role for virtues. So there is some hope left.

Literature

Anscombe, Gertrud (1958), 'Modern Moral Philosophy', *Philosophy*, 33(124): 1–19.
Aristotle (1977), *Politics*, Cambridge, MA/London: Loeb Classical Library.
Dreyfus, H. and Kelly, S.D. (2011), *All Things Shining: Reading the Western Classics to Find Meaning in a Secular Age*, New York: Free Press.
MacIntyre, Alasdair (1981), *After Virtue, A Study in Moral Theory*, Notre Dame, IN: University of Notre Dame Press.
Nietzsche, F. (AC) (1990) 'The Antichrist', in *Twilight of the Idols/The Antichrist*, trans. by R.J. Hollingdale, Penguin Books (original: *Der Antichrist*, in KSA vol. 6).
Nietzsche, F. (BGE) (1966) *Beyond Good and Evil*, trans. by W. Kaufmann, New York: Vintage (original: *Jenseits von Gut und Böse*, in KSA vol. 5).
Nietzsche, F. (D) (1982) *Daybreak*, trans. by R.J. Hollingdale, Cambridge University Press (original: *Morgenröthe*, in KSA vol. 3).
Nietzsche, F. (GM) (1969) *On the Genealogy of Morals*, trans. by W. Kaufmann, New York: Vintage (original: *Zur Genealogie der Moral*, in KSA vol. 5).
Nietzsche, F. (GS) (1974) *The Gay Science*, trans. by W. Kaufmann, New York: Vintage (original: *Die fröhliche Wissenschaf*, in KSA vol. 3).
Nietzsche, F. (HAH) (1986) II.2 WS: *Human, All Too Human*, vol. II, pt. 2 'The wanderer and his shadow', translated by R.J. Hollingdale, Cambridge University Press (original: *Menschliches, Allzumenschliches*. II.2 'Der Wanderer und sein Schatten', in KSA vol. 2).
Nietzsche, F. (KSA) (1988) *Kritische Studienausgabe in 15 banden*, G. Colli & M. Montinari (eds), Berlin/München: DTV.
Nietzsche, F. (TI) (1990) *Twilight of the Idols* In: Fr. Nietzsche, *Twilight of the Idols/The Antichrist*, trans. by R.J. Hollingdale, Penguin Books (original: *Götzendämmerung*, in KSA vol. 6).

Nietzsche, F. (SE) (1995) *Schopenhauer as Educator*, trans. by Richard T. Gray, Stanford University Press (original: *Schopenhauer als Erzieher* (Unzeitgemässe Betrachtungen III). in KSA vol. 1.

Nietzsche, F. (Unpublished Notes) trans. by the author from the original in KSA vol. 7–13.

Nietzsche, F. (Z) (1976) *Thus Spoke Zarathustra*, trans. by W. Kaufmann, New York: Penguin (original: *Also sprach Zarathustra*, in: KSA vol. 4).

Scheler, Max (1955), 'Zur Rehabilitierung der Tugend', in *Vom Umsturz der Werte: Abhandlungen und Aufsäätze. Gesammelte Werke Bd. 3*, 13–31, Bern: Francke.

Sloterdijk, Peter (2000), *Regels voor het Mensenpark*, Amsterdam: Boom.

Swanton, Christine (1998), 'Outline of a Nietzschean Virtue Ethics', *International Studies in Philosophy*, 30(3): 29–38.

Swanton, Christine (2003), *Virtue Ethics: A Pluralist View*, Oxford: Oxford University Press.

Tongeren, Paul van (2000), *Reinterpreting Modern Culture: An Introduction to Friedrich Nietzsche's Philosophy*, West Lafayette, IN: Purdue University Press.

Tongeren, Paul van (2002), 'Nietzsche's Greek Measure', *The Journal of Nietzsche Studies*, 24(1): 5–24.

Tongeren, Paul van (2010), ' "Ein Thier oder ein Gott", oder beides. Nietzsches Ueber Wahrheit und Lüüge im aussermoralischen Sinne und Aristoteles' Politik', *Nietzsche-Studien*, 39(1): 55–69.

Tongeren, Paul van (2012), 'Nietzsche's Questioning', *South African Journal of Philosophy*, 31(4): 692–701.

Zibis, Alexander-Maria (2007), *Die Tugend des Mutes: Nietzsches Lehre von der Tapferkeit*, Würzburg: Königshausen & Neumann.

Shame

In shame something is revealed that does not want to be seen, or should not be seen. When I feel ashamed, I have the feeling of being undressed and shown in a bad light. I can only be shown in a bad light as far as I don't want to be seen. The other sees my insecurity, clumsiness, my desire, or something else I don't want to show but have to acknowledge. In fact, I agree with the other person's presumed judgement. It is not even necessary that there is a real other who sees me. After all, I can also feel ashamed without there being someone else seeing me; or even if I know that the other person has long forgotten my stupidity, I can still feel ashamed of it.

The primary effect of that revelation is a loss of trust and alienation from the world, a fundamental lack of security. Shame is a feeling of distress. A very strong reaction, therefore, which also explains why memories of experiences of shame are so deep and are held on for so long.

Shame leads to 'submissive behaviour': the head is bent, the gaze is directed downwards, the arms hang powerlessly along the body. The revelation that has taken place apparently leads me to surrender myself: lifelessly surrendered to the power (and the gaze) of the other. That is remarkable. Although *something* of me is revealed, *I* feel distressed. Shame seems to be an experience of losing identity, an experience that relates to the character. The actual object of shame is not what I am ashamed of, but I am ashamed of the fact that it is something of mine, the way in which my personality becomes visible in it. I am not so much ashamed of my stupid or shameful act, but of my personality. While guilt is about an act, shame is about the person.

However, the two are more intertwined than this distinction suggests. Also, the experience of guilt requires that the person identifies as the actor. And the experience of shame makes clear how the person can be connected to an act against his or her will. I am ashamed to be a voyeur in someone else's eyes, which I became by getting caught looking through the keyhole. This act and the fact that I was seen turn me into what I do not want to be; I am bound to an act that alienates me from myself. The confusing nature of the experience of shame probably has to do with this distressing and expropriating effect of the revelation.

Shame is not only an effect of the revelation, but also a reaction to it, a defence against it. Strategies such as concealment, withholding, and distracting attention are used against the emerging or imminent upheaval.

When I am ashamed I try to hide myself: I put my hands before my eyes, try to sneak away, to become invisible (which again shows how not my action but my person is at stake). A good example is the stocks: it was used to put people to shame. Their punishment, however, was to make the natural reaction of those who were ashamed impossible. The way they were exhibited prevented them from doing what those who are ashamed usually do, and what little children do when they want to hide: they put their hands before their eyes assuming that if they cannot see, they cannot be seen either. Blushing, too, is such a concealment, and clearly shows the ambiguity that characterizes it: for this concealment reveals exactly that which it wants to conceal. Those who are ashamed often try to act normally in a conspicuous way. Hiding your face in your hands is a very visible way of trying to make yourself invisible.

Often shame is characterized by keeping quiet, by the refusal to speak about it. Psychiatrists and psychotherapists talk about the unproductive, destructive, paralysing and damaging effect of shame on mental health: 'Shame can be so overwhelming that people keep quiet for life', making psychotherapeutic treatment difficult or impossible! The patient is not really present, as it were; he or she has withdrawn him- or herself.

A third strategy is to do something about the thing that caused shame. Usually such a change is only possible through an illusion. This is therefore often what happens: the failed act or the shameful experience is endlessly re-experienced in an attempt to get a grip on it and, if possible, to make changes to it. Exaggeration in the representation of what happened can also be an attempt to trivialize what happened, in reality, and thus deny its seriousness. Perhaps this is also part of what everyone has experienced at one time or another: people who stumble first look around them and then go and look at the tile they stumble over in detail, or they tie their lace, as if they wanted to say: I didn't do anything crazy, but there was something wrong with that tile or those laces.

All these reactions, however, do not alter the fact that in the experience of shame something positive is discovered at the same time, that is, that I do not necessarily coincide with what has been revealed about me, or with the personality that was revealed. For no matter how much I endorse the viewer's judgement in my shame, at the same time I keep on resisting it or searching for how to relate to it. Apparently I don't entirely coincide with the person who was shown here, but I relate to him. I discover that I do not coincide with the person shown by the 'act'. Not only do I not coincide with the act, but not even with the person who acted, the person who showed himself in the act, or the person who became visible through that act or through the act as others perceived it. Perhaps we could say that shame makes me discover that the person I seemed to be is just a *persona*, a mask. Perhaps we should distinguish between the person and the self and use these terms to describe this difficult distinction.

We should not be satisfied with this 'discovery' too quickly. It doesn't help us regain what was expropriated. What we discover does not mean much. It may be that I discover that I am more than that which is suddenly naked and visible; but the thing with which I protected and concealed it has been taken from me, so that it no longer belongs to me, but to the others who see me. Although the experience of shame shows that the 'expropriation' also has a downside – since in that experience I also seem to distinguish myself from that expropriated self, and thus do not coincide with it – this does not mean that I can easily protect myself against the painful experience by, so to speak, shedding my skin and thereby escaping the judgement of others. For who am I when I am no longer kept together by my skin?

What is that 'other self' that can appear in the experience of shame? Presumably we only do justice to it if we recognize its unavailability. Shame then is to have the experience of 'another self', of which we simultaneously discover that we do not have it at our disposal, and that it is not capable of doing anything, that it is powerless. In this way we acknowledge that shame does indeed create an opportunity: there is the realization that I could be different, that in a way I am even different from how others perceive me, but that realization cannot be separated from the pain of shame, because the self discovers that it is powerless.

Powerless or at the mercy of others. The one who is ashamed, I think, is indeed at the mercy of others: not only of the other person who turns him or her into someone he or she does not want to be, but also of the help we can get in our powerlessness. Parents can sometimes turn their children's experiences of shame to good use by covering or embracing them. Socrates comes to the aid of the interlocutors who were ashamed of him by sharing in their desperation.

The Fall of Man is a story about shame. Adam and Eve discovered that they were naked and covered themselves out of shame. Their expulsion from Paradise is the beginning of human history. Humans are the kind of creature that is ashamed: we distinguish ourselves from the other animals by a self – which is powerless handed over to the mercy of others. Fortunately Adam and Eve were together, and on most pictures of their expulsion they at least walk out of Paradise hand in hand.

VI VIRTUE ETHICS IN A DISENCHANTED WORLD

Aristotelian virtue ethics is based on an optimistic concept of nature: nature is well constructed. This applies to human nature with its natural desires, and it also applies to the world of which humans are a part. Both elements are of great significance for that form of virtue ethics. Virtues can be understood as cultivations, optimizations of something innate, something we can rely on. Since the all-encompassing nature is well constructed, humankind's natural desire cannot be pointless or aimless either. In the ethics of Aristotle, it is constantly clear how self-evident that is to him.

Later, Hellenistic and especially Stoic ethics reinforced this element. Aristotle could still acknowledge that besides his own moral quality, coincidental circumstances also influenced the extent to which one flourishes. Good practice (that is: a virtuous life) does not guarantee an optimal result. One must also be a little lucky to become happy (see Chapter II.3). For the Stoics the circumstances do not really matter. According to them, what matters is that you conform to nature, to the nature within yourself, and eventually to nature in general. Whether you do that as an emperor or as a slave does not make much difference. Luck and bad luck only exist for those who do not conform to nature, but put their own particular interests first. After all, chance only relates to the things that this personal interest is aimed at. Virtue consists in knowing that these personal interests do not matter, but that happiness consists in becoming *homologous* to nature, coinciding with nature, wanting nothing but what the natural course of things has in store for you and becoming indifferent to everything else.

The view of nature that emerges from this – and which we, to a lesser extent, find in Aristotle – sees nature as a good order. That is why we call the greater whole *kosmos*, which means: 'jewel'! Human nature is part of this, meaning that we can assume that humankind's natural desire is itself meaningful: the happiness we seek is attainable for us; we are suited to what we are aiming for; and that which we – actually, deeply – strive for really brings us to completion.

This view of nature seems to be far behind us. Although ...? Most nature films still evoke admiration for this impressive spectacle that, though it may seem cruel at times, does in the end form a beautiful whole. Yet something has indeed changed. According to the Stoics, if nature didn't do what you wanted or thought was right, you had to learn to see that that was down to you. Nature is good, but people sometimes acquire the wrong preferences. Nowadays it seems rather the other way around: when we realize that we like nature, this is usually only the case because nature does what we want it to do. However, if that same nature produces floods, earthquakes and atrocities, we see our mistake. For the Stoics our personal desires were considered illusions; for us the perception of nature as good and beautiful is an illusory projection of our desires in relation to nature.

And we have the same distrust in our own natural desires, or at least in those of others. People can (and often will) pursue something that is bad for them, sometimes even what will ruin them. And that is not so much because they are alienated from their nature, but rather because that nature itself does not serve as a good compass (any more).

In a way, this view had already come into the world with Christianity, as we saw (Chapter IV.3.2). Nature is a fallen nature and therefore humans are – as the Heidelberg Catechism says – 'totally incapable of any good and inclined to all evil'. Therefore, all of ethics after the Reformation will focus on the restriction of that nature. From then on, ethics somehow always begins with the prohibitions of a law that sets limits, that is: limits to natural desires. And even before the Reformation, in Catholic Christianity, the theological virtues testified to the imperfection of nature (cf. Chapter IV.3): humans do not attain perfection without the grace of God, which is, after all, an infringement of nature.

In Christianity, the unreliability of nature is still relatively small: it concerns fallen nature, and not the original nature created by God. Modern science has set this notion of creation aside. What we have left is a nature that is ingeniously constructed (and that undoubtedly still inspires wonder, or even admiration, among individual scientists), but that ultimately lacks any moral quality in itself. Nature is a matter of fact for the scientist (and for scientifically thinking modern humankind). We try to control nature to make it fit our desires better; desires that in themselves are not good or bad, but that are simply there. In dealing with nature, we must build dikes, natural parks, laboratories and – as far as *human* nature is concerned – establish rights and organize legal means of force to ensure that we comply with them. The humanities (including the social sciences) have also become a kind of natural sciences. They study human nature in order to achieve greater control over it.

What does this development mean for ethics in general and for Aristotelian virtue ethics in particular?

1 Ethics and (human) sciences

Scientific knowledge will undeniably influence ethics. This was already the case for Aristotle's ethics, and it will only be more true in our time, in which scientific knowledge has developed so much further.

Aristotle himself constantly uses his knowledge of facts in his ethical theory: the teleological model of human life that I mentioned already, the view that life is directed at and suited for a purpose that is already given in that life itself, goes, according to him, not only for human life, but for all life, for all nature. Aristotle sees it as an empirical fact that directs his biological theory as much as his ethics. Of course, for him, the separation of scientific and philosophical knowledge, as we use it nowadays, did not exist, but from our perspective we can only interpret his thinking as a mix of science and philosophy. He also regularly uses scientific knowledge in his ethical research, including that which we can regard as a kind of 'human sciences *avant la lettre*'. For example, when he questions what the purpose of human life actually is, or better, what *eudaimonia*, 'happiness', as we call that purpose, actually stands for, his answer to this question starts with the results of a kind of social-scientific research. If you look at what people actually consider to be the purpose of their lives, you will see that it differs from group to group. He organizes the data into three types: some find their purpose in pleasure, others in the recognition of their contribution to society and a third group believes that knowledge and understanding are the highest form of happiness. His philosophical-ethical interpretation of this data also contains many elements that are based on experience and contain empirical claims: propositions that, in principle, should be testable through empirical scientific research. If Aristotle, for example, states that virtue is a disposition, he then explains that such a disposition is created by the development of a habit: whoever always acts in a certain way – initially forced or stimulated by external entities and means – will eventually build up a habit of acting in this way, a habit, which, if gradually internalized, becomes a disposition. Our character would thus be a set of dispositions, ethics a matter of character, and character a matter of education and practice.

Something like this asks for scientific assessment and therefore for an exchange between philosophy (ethics) and science. In a 2008 book (*Experiments in Ethics*) the British-Ghanaian-American philosopher Kwame Anthony Appiah described in various ways the importance of such an exchange, especially between ethics and experimental psychology. According to him, there is no reason for any reservation in this, or for fear that empirical testing would undermine the theses of (virtue) ethics. He elaborates on three points in particular.

First, he describes the already-mentioned role of character. Virtue ethics centres on that role and thus seems to assume that there is indeed something like a stable character, a set of dispositions that despite varying situations causes people to keep acting in a similar manner, determined by that character: it is supposed that friendly people react to what happens to them in a friendly way, no matter the circumstances. However, social-scientific research (as carried out in particular by John Doris) seems to call into question the existence of such fixed dispositions, and seems to show that our actions are determined by circumstances to a much greater extent than they are by any character traits. Whether people help each other – an experiment has shown – seems to be more influenced by random circumstances (whether or not they have just found a coin in a telephone kiosk, or they smell the scent of freshly baked bread) than by their character. But instead of undermining the thesis of virtue ethics, it nuances and refines it: virtuous traits are not so abundant that you will find them in any random sample; even though a character trait will usually manifest itself in actions, there remains a difference between someone's character (the person he or she is) and what he or she does; moreover, a virtuous trait can be present to varying degrees; and above all: a virtuous person is aware of precisely this role of circumstances and – as much as possible – anticipates them, tries to avoid bad conditions and create good ones.

Second, moral intuitions play an important role in all of ethics. The ethicist would be rather powerless if he or she could not appeal to a feeling of justice, a desire for a meaningful life, an elementary awareness of the importance of the consequences of your actions, or the intuitive belief that a world in which more people suffer less can be called better, and so on. Psychological research has revealed that many of these intuitions do not so much exist on the basis of a well-ordered nature, but are influenced by irrelevant factors and can therefore easily be manipulated. By formulating an alternative, you can largely determine the answers of the respondents. Research shows that people will, for example, prefer a decision that is likely to save 20 per cent of the population to one that is likely to sacrifice 80 per cent of the population. So you know how to present it, depending on whether you want to implement or stop the decision. If and insofar as our moral intuitions are determined by such manipulable conditions, they can indeed hardly produce a reliable argument. On the other hand, scientific knowledge of factors that determine our intuitions can help us test those intuitions and learn to distinguish between more and less reliable options. If you know that your intuitive reaction is determined by the way the message is presented, you might confront different formulations. Then you will be better informed and still be able to make a decision based on your intuitions. Ultimately, we will have to choose which moral feelings we do or do not follow, and we cannot do so on the basis of explanations of how they arise. We can only use these explanations in the reasons we are giving, which are themselves at least partly based on moral feelings. Social-scientific research does not take away the role of intuitions, but offers opportunities to make better use of them, by using them more critically.

The constructive connection between ethics and (human) science appears to be strongest with regard to the third point mentioned by Appiah, which particularly affects every form of ethics that relies on the nature of humankind. Virtue ethics sees the virtuous life as an extension of natural desire; and in a certain sense this also applies to utilitarianism, which tries to indicate how to satisfy the most (actual, natural) preferences of the greatest number. Scientific research shows that nature has always been to a certain extent cultural, or culturally determined. There is no 'pure' form of nature, because it has been shaped over the course of history. What we see as 'nature' is a moment in an ongoing process that is determined by both biological evolution and cultural history. On the one hand, this seems to threaten any universalist pretence of ethics; on the other hand science itself sometimes tends to explain the different cultural patterns on the basis of an underlying nature. It then becomes reductionist because, for example, it reduces all morality to the survival strategy of species, individuals or their genes. Instead, a real collaboration between ethics and science can, and must, help us avoid both naive universalism and equally naive reductionism. Cross-cultural 'modules' (a term coined by American psychologists Jonathan Haidt and Craig Joseph) can be identified, which we also recognize in the major ethical theories: justice, reciprocity, recognizing the importance of the consequences of your actions, the role of a certain social hierarchy, the importance of purity and the admiration for exemplary persons are some examples of what we find in the great ethical traditions of eudaimonism, deontological ethics, contractualism and utilitarianism. Not all modules play an equally important role in every theory, but most theories contain several modules and each of them is of central importance at least somewhere. The most important lesson we can draw from this is that no single ethical theory is perfect in itself, but that they offer different perspectives that stem from deep layers of our always culturally determined nature (cf. also Chapter II.2).

Scientific knowledge of (human) nature and empirical testing of ethical theories therefore in no way undermine ethics. And how could they? After all, ethical theories were invented by people whose nature is mapped out by these sciences. Moreover, we have to know the nature of the human being about whose life we want to speak in an evaluative and normative sense! Neither norms nor ideals make sense if they do not fit with the nature of the people who should be aiming at them. Appiah rightly points out that it is strange to speak of the need for a connection between ethics and science: the two have never actually been separated: not with Aristotle, nor with Descartes, nor with Hume, nor with Mill. Only Kant is not mentioned here by Appiah, and that probably has to do with the following.

There is, in fact, a problem – one that I think Appiah is ignoring. He rightly shows that scientific knowledge of human beings is important to ethics, which seeks to discuss the conditions under which human life can be described as good and just. However, his interest only consists in checking whether what ethics says fits with what we can scientifically establish about the nature of humankind. However critical this question may be, ultimately the whole enterprise remains within a paradigm characterized by what I call 'trust in nature'. Knowledge of human nature is used to adjust, adapt, if necessary correct, theses about the good life. The underlying idea seems to be that ethics must in any case fit with nature; but probably even more than that.

The question of to what extent stable character traits exist and what their role is in the way that people respond to common situations, does not in any case contest the assumption that kindness, helpfulness, bravery etc. are virtues that fit with human nature. The acknowledgement that moral intuitions must be critically tested because not everything that presents itself as such indeed testifies to pure moral feeling, and that perhaps there is not even such a thing at all, does not alter the fact that in the always culturally determined human nature there seems to be a sense of good and justice, even if this can be distorted. The discovery of moral modules that are found cross-culturally reinforces this idea of a natural moral awareness and provides perspective for the idea of morality based in nature. The question of the basis of morality, i.e. the question on what grounds we actually call those things 'good' that morality presents to us as such, may not be posed explicitly, but it is implicitly answered – at least in part – by the aforementioned trust in nature.

This is not surprising: throughout the ages we find the same thought with most philosophers. Not only the premodern thinkers, but the modern empiricists and the widespread utilitarianism, too, ultimately find the answer to the question of why we call something good in the nature of moral feeling or of human desire. Kant seems to be an exception (and perhaps for that reason was not mentioned by Appiah): he contrasted morality, as a demand made by reason, with nature. This makes Kant not only an exponent of the Enlightenment, but also and especially of the Reformation, which emphasized the Fall and thus the decaying nature of humankind. According to Kant, any form of ethics that starts with our natural desire ignores the possibility that this very desire may be thoroughly wrong: 'Eudaimonism in ethics', he writes, 'leads to "euthanasia of morality"' (MdS, 506). Therefore, we should not follow our nature, but obey reason. But however much he places the demand of reason against the power of nature, Kant (immediately at the beginning of his 'Groundwork for the metaphysics of morals'; part I, section 5) cannot escape an appeal to nature, in which he sees reason as the most important force, stronger than the force of (other) natural desires.

The question I would like to raise in response to Appiah's position is this: doesn't this confidence in nature – even if it only expresses itself in the demand that morality should correspond to nature, and thus to our scientific knowledge of it – still imply a moral qualification of nature, a belief that nature is ultimately well constructed? And isn't that exactly the kind of belief that science would like to correct in us? Scientifically speaking, nature is neither good nor bad. Undeniably, knowledge of nature remains a prerequisite for anyone who wants to achieve something with regard to nature, but whether what we want is good or not, we cannot – it seems – derive from nature or our knowledge of it.

Aristotle could, since he – as we have already seen – started from a concept of nature according to which nature itself was already morally qualified: nature is well constructed. However, from the moment that modern science 'neutralizes' nature in terms of morality, we lack a basis for our trust in nature. This does not mean that ethics should not be interested in what science teaches us about nature. But to the extent that one bases one's ethics on that scientifically understood nature, one is inevitably guilty of the fallacy that leaps from 'being' to 'being good' (and possibly from 'is' to 'ought'). Some modern naturalistic theories go as far as to use some kind of survival instinct, coupled with some form of necessary cooperation, as the ground on which an ethical system can be built. Some scientists are starting to believe that they can now take over the task of ethics, and are starting to formulate ethical propositions themselves based on their knowledge of nature. Appiah does not do all this, but neither does he fundamentally question the paradigm in which nature functions as the basis of morality.

Could that be possible at all? Can we live without that trust in nature? It seems a difficult task. Can virtue ethics help us with this task too?

2 Scientific knowledge and interpreting meaning

Modern ethics likes to base itself upon facts. That goes for a naturalistic ethics that is based on actual human nature, and it even goes, in a certain sense, for the anti-naturalistic ethics of Kant, who after all invokes 'the fact of reason'.

It will be clear – at least to everyone who has read Chapter II – that the hermeneutical perspective of this book points in a different direction. Ethics as a philosophical discipline is an *interpretation* of the *meaning* of facts. No matter how important factual knowledge may be – and Appiah rightly points this out – its meaning can only be deduced if people have secretly inserted it into facts to begin with. Such hidden presuppositions are only possible if they enjoy the force of self-evidence. No one will doubt that people, like other animals, have survival as their goal. But philosophy, and thereby also ethics, has the task to question self-evident facts. Why would you want to survive? Are there no ideals for which I would sacrifice even my life? And what does it mean if they do not exist (any more)? But most of all: how should I survive?

That does not alter the fact that philosophy must also place its own self-evidence under scrutiny. And the development of our culture, in which the sciences play an important role, has certainly helped us to strip the presuppositions of a premodern culture of their self-evidence. We can probably no longer trust with the same self-evidence that nature is well constructed, even though we have established that scientists themselves sometimes still hold on to that belief. In contrast to the Greek admiration for the cosmos stands the modern awareness of chaos; in contrast to the opening of the Gospel of John – 'In the beginning was the Word (*logos*), and the Word was with God, and the Word was God' – there is Nietzsche's parody of it: 'In the beginning was the madness, and the madness was by God!' (HAH II.1 AOM, 22). And so we must ask ourselves, how to think about ethics without the self-evident and reliable basis of a good and meaningful nature? The – typically modern – deontological ethics of Kant may still formulate duties independent of nature, but this is not an option for virtue ethics. Virtue ethics, after all, does not put the good against, but in line with, natural desire. But how can this still be possible, if that desire originates from a nature that is not 'well constructed'?

To work this out, we should not talk about the confrontation of ethics (philosophy) and science, about the confrontation of moral meaning and factual knowledge, but about those between different interpretations of nature, and thus ultimately about different cosmologies, metaphysical designs, and the question of how ethics and especially virtue ethics relate to them. Is a form of ethics that sees good life as an extension of natural desire, that sees human completion as the optimal realization of what is potentially given in human nature still possible in the context of an interpretation that no longer sees nature as a good order?

It is not possible to elaborate such metaphysics in this book. Nevertheless, in order to present the question as pressingly as possible, I would like to present (in sections 3 and 4) a position that provides an impressive, totally different, modern interpretation of human nature. Here I turn to Paul Moyaert who has presented Jacques Lacan's elaboration of Freudian psychoanalysis and its ethical implications in several publications. In this psychoanalysis we find science, hermeneutics and ethics together: it contains the empirical facts of the clinical experience, but these are interpreted and generalized in interpretative schemes, and explicitly associated with ethics by Lacan and Moyaert themselves. According to Moyaert, Lacan works according to Aristotle's classical scheme: moral experience is explained on the basis of a theory of the human psyche, which itself fits within a contemporary interpretation of (human) reality as a whole. However, this *Weltanschauung* and the psychology that suits it are now radically different from those of Aristotle's time and, as a result, ethics, that is to say the interpretation of moral experience, can no longer remain on the Aristotelian track. The challenge for virtue ethics, which sees morality as an extension of natural desire, is undeniable. I will clarify this in section 5 and I will try to respond to this challenge in sections 6 and 7. Sections 3 to 5 are based on Paul Moyaert's work – or at least my interpretation of it.

3 The structure of desire

Unlike the scientists I referred to earlier, Lacan does not seem a naturalist in the strong sense of the word. He does not reduce psychological reality to a biological or other kind of natural substrate. He does not reduce meaning to facts. Although humans are a species of animal, what distinguishes them from other animals is exactly what is interesting about humankind. Animals have instincts, but in humans something happens to those instincts, turning them from biological forces to psychological desires, and turning the reality of nature into a world of meanings. According to Lacan, there is inevitably a disruptive element in this world of meaning.

What 'happens' in the transition from natural instincts to psychological desires can be summarized as a prohibition. Psychoanalysis usually calls this prohibition the incest prohibition, which at the very least provides a clarifying metaphor: intercourse with the mother is excluded so that a desire for a partner may arise. This prohibition restricts the natural forces by law and transforms them into a desire that is bound by rules. The law distinguishes between what is and what is not permitted and creates regulated relationships. Through this law, animals become human beings, solitary animals become members of a group, or the herd becomes a community.

With this law the community comes into being and that which already makes it a human community according to Aristotle (see Chapter I.5):

the language in which one can communicate about meanings, about what is permitted and what is not; about what is good and bad, beautiful and ugly, and so on. The reference to Aristotle cannot conceal the fact that there is an important difference between both views. The fact that I point to the resemblance is only to highlight the difference more clearly. In Aristotle's work, we saw a natural development in which people – that is, animals that have *logos* – form a meaningful community. Psychoanalysis – just like Nietzsche (cf. GM, II.16) – does not see this community as the completion of a natural growth process, but as the product of a fracture. This difference will be important for ethics: for Aristotle, moral goodness consists in perfecting what is natural. From this other perspective, on the other hand, i.e. from the perspective of Nietzsche, Freud and Lacan, morality, which is only possible within this human world, will always have a deep and essential line of fracture. This break will feel like a tension within our moral sensibility: the tension between the pre-moral and amoral dynamics of the original nature on the one hand and the moral desire created by prohibition on the other. For no matter how much the law draws a line, the other side of the line, that which precedes the break, has not disappeared, as we shall see.

Psychoanalysis interprets the world of humankind, as it is created by the prohibition, as a 'symbolic order'. Characteristic of the symbolic order is the language and that which becomes possible through language, namely articulation, translation and interpretation. These three can be summarized in the concept of 'substitution'. One word can be translated with, or explained by (and in that sense 'substituted by') another word. One commodity can be exchanged for another: money is also a means of communication and economy is a symbolic system. The same scheme is true in a broader sense: we can explain the value of something and its meaning, we can compare and choose on that basis, we can negotiate and try to find a common denominator for different preferences – these are all ways in which the symbolic order shows itself as a 'system of equivalence'. Everything in the world has a meaning, and all these meanings have their place in a system, in which they can be explained or interpreted. And each interpretation replaces in a sense the thing that is interpreted by the interpretation.

Not everything can be substituted, however. First of all, hermeneutics reminds us that the interpretation can never replace the thing that is interpreted (the interpretation of the poem cannot replace the poem) and that complete equivalence is therefore impossible. Second, psychoanalysis points to meanings that escape interpretation in a much more fundamental way. Sometimes things can acquire a meaning for people that is not an expression of a personal preference, but that imposes itself with absolute force. Such meanings cannot be translated or explained. When Montaigne tries to explain why Étienne de la Boétie is an irreplaceable friend for him, it turns out he can't. His famous essay on friendship is full of comparisons, but it only seems to make clear that nothing compares to it. This friendship turns out to be incomparable: 'If I were pressed to say why I love him, I feel that my only reply could be: "Because it was he, because it was I"' (Montaigne 1958: 97). Here we come to the point where we cannot or do not want to answer the question of why we are acting in a certain way: 'Why? Well, just because.' At this point, people can become martyrs. For example, Luther is said to have stated in Worms 'Here I stand, I can do no other'.

However, this is not yet fully in conflict with the system of equivalence of the symbolic order. This system also depends on a few elements from which it is structured. After all, we usually accept that someone unconditionally binds him- or herself to a specific person, or that someone chooses truth over everything else, even over his or her own interest. Even if we disagree with someone, we can understand that something is 'sacred' to him or her. The sacred is itself one of the meanings by which the symbolic order is structured.

At the same time, however, the limit of that symbolic order and of the community it makes possible appears. Luther was excommunicated because of his remark. People can become isolated because of their absolute commitment to a cause. If we offer help to someone who no longer wants to live after the death of his partner, it may seem insulting to the person concerned, because we deny the absolute nature of that relationship. This is not always a matter of time. Antigone, who wants to bury her brother at all costs (her marriage, her life and that of her fiancée and her mother, her own happiness as well as that of the political community), shows that there is no clear boundary to be drawn between loyalty and heroism on the one hand and madness and fanaticism on the other. We should also consider the danger of fanaticism that is tied to theological virtues (cf. Chapter IV.4.1).

We might call Antigone a pathological case. But if it was only pathology, the tragedy wouldn't still resonate with us. Psychoanalysis rightly sees pathology not as an exception, but as the manifestation of something latent in every human being, and that, according to Freud, causes 'uneasiness in culture'. In pathology, there is a dramatic outburst which normally is only a certain restlessness, a slight uneasiness – or in the words of Willem Elsschot's famous poem *The Marriage*: that 'melancholy, which no-one can explain, which comes at evening time when it is sleep you need'.

The absolute attachment to something or someone shows the aforementioned fracture, and the fact that the desire is shaped by the prohibition of a preceding dynamic. Human desire does not only contain the energy of that preceding force, but also the resistance against its suppression. This resistance shows itself in that unreasonable and incomprehensible attachment to something, an attachment that cannot be explained, justified or mediated. That which precedes the meaningful order infiltrates that order as a strange element: incomprehensible, nonsensical, bizarre. The resistance to the prohibition, by which the moral desire remains connected with the amoral force from which it originates, is shown in the way in which the desire can surrender itself to an object, a person, or a sign for something else. Through our entering into the symbolic order we are cut off from that 'preceding', which Lacan calls 'the real'. But that reality enters the symbolic order in the form of an object that on the one hand has an absolute meaning, but on the other hand is not 'meaning' in the actual sense of the word. Its 'absoluteness' shows that this 'meaning' has become detached ('absolute' is derived from the Latin *absolvere*, to detach). Such a 'meaning' is no longer part of a set of meaningful references and can therefore not be translated, nor interpreted. The fact that this attachment can be felt in the guts betrays its origin outside the world of meaning. The object that receives this absolute 'meaning' can therefore only appear from the symbolic order as if randomly and the attachment to it can only be unreasonable and incomprehensible, even to the person him- or herself.

After all, that person too is a construction within the symbolic order. Whoever says 'I' participates in that order, in which saying 'I' has a meaning, in which 'I' and 'you' and 'they' are distinct positions, in which relations are bound to certain rules, and so on. What 'I' am and who I am can only be explained within the world of meaning, of which we are part by the breach with the real that nevertheless permeates it. The 'I' does not precede the system of meanings within which I function. So 'I' comes about through this breach with a preceding world which therefore also remains inaccessible to me.

It is important to distinguish this theory from a naturalistic position, which would state that the 'I' is only an epiphenomenon of what on a deeper level is the functioning of genes or the brain, or of whatever. Such a position would suggest that if I say 'I', that 'actually' is only an echo of what 'in fact' is an anonymous event. Individuality would 'actually' be an illusion, however much it is cherished. Psychoanalysis suggests something else. It does not reduce our individuality to something infra-individual, it does not dismiss it as an illusion, but gives it a different explanation. It states that my saying 'I' has always been part of the world of meanings, which has always been a shared world, one in which everything is basically interchangeable. But there is something in my 'I' that isolates me from that community, something that singularizes me. However, this is something that I cannot explain myself, something that I do not have, but that rather has me. That is why psychoanalysis prefers to speak of 'singularity' rather than 'individuality'. Lacan uses the term 'extimacy' to indicate that I am in the core not myself. My soul is not mine and I cannot reach it myself.

For that reason, it can be misleading to speak of 'resistance to the prohibition', as I did before. 'Resistance' suggests that there is 'someone' who resists. However, this 'someone' only comes about through the prohibition and is, as it were, equal to the resistance. And the same goes for desire. In that desire and in that resistance lies that which does not fit into it, because desire and resistance only come about precisely through its exclusion.

4 The ethics of psychoanalysis

All this has important consequences for the fulfilment of desire, and for the form of ethics that seeks to situate itself in line with desire. In a way, Lacan continues the line of Aristotle. Unlike Kant, who contrasts morality (of pure practical reason) with nature, for Lacan morality is still an extension of nature, but in this 'extension' there is a fracture. The nature that precedes this is not itself a meaningful order and therefore not morally qualified; it is only through the prohibition that it becomes so. Because desire remains connected with this nature that precedes the prohibition, that is to say with that 'meaningless' and amoral nature from which we are separated by the prohibition, fulfilment of desire now seems to be impossible. After all, it is attached to what it excludes, and by the exclusion from which it comes about. Thus, paradoxically, the impossibility of fulfilling the desire seems to be the condition for its existence.

Of course, that does not mean that we are condemned to constant dissatisfaction and discontent. Elsschot's 'melancholy', too, came 'at evening time'. Within the order of desire, all kinds of goals can be realized, at least for those who follow the rules of that order. These rules mean, as we saw, that every goal is fundamentally interchangeable. In a certain sense there may even be 'absolute goals', but only to the extent that they are accepted in the community, for example as the prevailing views. As long as, for example, religion has not yet completely disappeared from culture, we can 'understand' that some things – even seemingly useless things like a headscarf or the difference between animals with and without split hoofs – are 'sacred' to some people. This acceptance, however, is contingent and is threatened from the moment it has to justify itself. We then see the fundamental gap between desire and fulfilment.

We have seen (in Chapter II.3) that in ethics 'happiness' is indeed referred to as the complete fulfilment of desire. We can describe the problem psychoanalysis points out to us in terms of the relationship between desire, happiness and the good. The fourth term I use is pleasure, because it plays an important role in the relationship between the other terms. In a form of ethics based on desire, pleasure will in any case be linked to happiness; according to many it is a sign of happiness, according to some it is even its content. In Aristotelian ethics, these four clearly belong together. Happiness is the name for the highest good, which consists in the optimal fulfilment of (well understood) desire, which is necessarily experienced as pleasurable and obviously only possible in the context of a (political) community. Lacan seems to problematize this connection on several points.

First, he seems to identify 'happiness' and 'pleasure', be it in a way that distinguishes him not only from Aristotle, but also from Plato and from hedonism as well. For Aristotle, pleasure is something that is attached to the successful activity in which happiness exists (cf. Chapter II.3.1). Anyone who does something that 'succeeds' will experience it as pleasant. Whoever succeeds in his life as a whole is happy and enjoys it. With this he seems to distance himself from Plato who sees pleasure rather as a dangerous temptation, by which we are distracted from the good. However, Aristotle, too, indicates that pleasure cannot be the criterion of happiness, as hedonism states, because even actions that do not make someone happy can 'succeed' and be enjoyable. Acting well will be experienced as pleasant, but that does not make every pleasant act a good one. Aristotle thus gives happiness – that is to say, the fulfilment of desire – a certain content. That content is an activity, and the pleasure is attached to its unobstructed and successful execution. Hedonism denies that happiness has a certain content and states that, on the contrary, it only exists in the experience of pleasure. Lacan is on the side of Aristotle (and opposes hedonism) insofar as he believes that pleasure is linked to a specific content, but he is on the side of Plato (and opposed to Aristotle) insofar as he believes that pleasure is easily alienated from good. For it is connected to the object that owes its significance to the real, that is to say: to that which is excluded by the order of the community and the good.

According to Lacan, that happiness/pleasure, the complete fulfilment of desire, is not only practically difficult, but fundamentally impossible to realize, because that desire arises from the exclusion of what it desires. The complete fulfilment would therefore be the death of desire. Happiness thus seems to be excluded. But apart from the link between desire and happiness, the link between happiness and good, too, is broken. For the good refers to a shared world of meanings, while desire and happiness, to which it is directed, are attached to something that does not care about that world of meaning. In everyday reality we see this last break all too clearly. Where the attachment takes the shape of an unbridled fanaticism, it is not limited by moral laws or by the interests of the community, not even by personal interests. While the desire in the context of Aristotle is fundamentally involved in that which is good, and good for you, it seems to Lacan to be constantly threatened by its involvement in that which excludes and destroys you. Again: this does not mean that desire always goes against what is right. However, it remains marked by the resistance to the prohibition that establishes it, and in that it remains connected with the opposite of what it seeks.

Perhaps we can summarize it like this: there is no meaningful connection between the world of meaning in which we live and the meaningless reality of the real from which that world of meaning nevertheless originates and to which it remains attached.

The latter formulation reminds us of (but is certainly not identical with) the Kantian distinction between the phenomenal and the noumenal world, that is: between the world as it appears to us and the world as it is in itself, apart from our perception or knowledge of it. We can only say something about the phenomenal world, because our language inevitably uses the forms and categories by which that world is constructed. We inevitably experience reality in terms of time and space and can only know it in terms of unity and multiplicity, cause and effect, possibility and necessity, etc. But these forms and categories do not belong to reality as it is in itself, regardless of how we experience it. It would also be a mistake to apply these categories to the relationship between these 'two worlds'. The noumenal reality is not the ground or cause of the phenomenal world.

However, the latter is not entirely true for the relation of what in psychoanalysis is called the real and the symbolic order. There is indeed a relationship between the two, although it is not a fundamental or meaningful relationship either. The real is in no way a foundation of the symbolic. The latter does arise from the former, namely through separation and prohibition; and the former infiltrates into the latter, namely in the form of disruption. So the relation is negative on both sides.

This negativity gives the theory a tragic quality, as we find it in Nietzsche's thoughts on Greek pessimism. The world of meaning has no foundation, human desire has no destination, under every construction of order lies chaos. Every meaning we experience can be futile nonsense. To use a metaphor of Nietzsche: the human situation is that of someone sleeping on the back of a tiger (PT). Psychoanalysis adds that it is also impossible to sleep quietly, i.e. to withdraw into the relatively safe world of meaning. For in this world the memory of its groundlessness inevitably appears, and it does so at the core of our own activity, that is, in that which normally may seem innocent in one's lifestyle or friendships, but which can easily become pathological in the fanatical attachment to a random object.

5 The challenge for ethics

It will be clear that this alternative interpretation of the human condition poses a major challenge to ethics. As beings of meaning, humans remain in their core attached to something that does not fit in any world of meaning. As moral beings, we remain tied to something that cannot be morally justified or explained in any way.

According to Moyaert, all existing ethical theories are bound to fail because of this abyss underneath our morality and our rationality. The moral being is not autonomous, or in other words: its rational autonomy remains itself supported by an endless heteronomy. And this heteronomy cannot be traced back to a rational order or a God, nor to the other who appeals to us and calls upon us. It is within us, but we cannot reach it ourselves. Moyaert connects the notion of 'human dignity' with loneliness: that which makes 'me' irreplaceable is something that escapes the world of meanings in which I could share with others, exchange and understand that which controls me with others.

There is no natural order to which we might conform, since order, the meaningful world, is created only by the law that separates humans from that which has no place in that order, but to which they at the same time remains attached. Even our own desire cannot guide us, for it remains defined by that which excludes it. Moyaert points out that free association (an essential element in the psychoanalytic cure) is always a frightening affair, because we fear that our conscious desires are somehow linked to those we do not want to know.

Neither one's own happiness, nor the common good, nor the agreements made with others, nor a universal law of reason can justify or explain why something or someone can acquire absolute meaning in the life of a human being. Or, to put it in the milder words that keep us out of pathology: none of these theories can explain why the absolute obligation of reason sometimes disappears into indifference or why happiness fails, even when all desires seem fulfilled.

Freud referred to the inevitable uneasiness in culture that is not dispelled when that same culture becomes a little more permissive; Nietzsche stated that it is superficial to think that humans strive for happiness (TI, Maxims and Arrows 12), and called humans the most pathological of all animals (AC, 14), because we have become detached from our instincts and therefore inevitably continue to look for what is withheld from us precisely because of this search. Whether this latent disease leads to a pathological illness is determined by chance. For the boundary between order and that from which it is separated is not itself bound to rationality.

In short, the challenge of the interpretation of the human condition by Lacanian psychoanalysis comes down to this: how could ethics ever do justice to a condition that makes that all of ethics (indeed, every meaning) is undermined by that which makes it possible? How can a form of ethics ever do justice to the profound tension that characterizes human moral sensitivity?

6 Can ethics provide answers?

We have already seen (e.g. in section 1 of this chapter) why we cannot expect everything from a single ethical approach. Different ethical systems are elaborations of different moral 'modules', of different aspects of moral experience. Only taken together could they give a more or less complete picture of our moral condition. However, the psychoanalytical interpretation of the human condition seems to problematize all ethical perspectives.

In this section and the next, I will try to formulate an ethical answer to the challenge. It cannot be a matter of 'solving' or removing the described tension in humankind's moral sensibility. After all, it proved to be constitutive of human existence, at least in the interpretation I am now taking as a starting point. Even less can I pretend to add a new ethical theory to the existing theories. But perhaps the idea of life as an art still offers the possibility of supplementing virtue ethics with a reflection that is in line with the indicated tense moral human condition and that can nevertheless help us to deal with it.

To this end, I reformulate this tense condition as follows: we are determined in our core, in our deepest commitments, in our closest ties, our strongest attachments by something we cannot reach ourselves. The question for ethics is, whether it can still give this profound alienation a place in our lives, whether it can explain whether and how we can, in a certain sense, make this alienating thing 'our own', how we can feel somewhat 'at home' in this condition that inevitably seems to make us displaced persons.

This problem is related to an experience that may be more 'familiar' to many (however alienating that familiar experience may be): you have done something of which you are ashamed, something you abhor, something you did not want to do, but that you did yourself. You have deceived someone, or you have shown yourself in your greatest vanity – everyone can fill in their own experiences. The comparison may seem unfair in that it concerns experiences of aspects of yourself that you explicitly condemn, from which you distance yourself, while that is not at all the case in the deep attachments that psychoanalysis referred to. In my opinion, however, the difference is not crucial. Even in these experiences, we realize at the same time that we cannot really distance ourselves from the aspects of ourselves that we condemn. It was I myself who committed the deceit, who showed my vanity; I am someone who does such things. Therefore the shame we feel is more important than our condemnation.

Shame is probably largely determined by my acknowledgement that the condemned aspect is not just an act I have caused, but it is part of who I am. In shame I feel naked, shown to others as I am. Experiences of shame, or dreams in which one does or experiences something that makes one feel ashamed, often have to do with nudity. Although I do not coincide with my nudity, it does show me as I am. In literature, the difference between guilt and shame is indeed determined in this way: guilt would relate to an act, but shame to the personality of the offender. I can distance myself from an act I have made; I can promise and intend never to do it again, but I cannot do that to what I am. And yet there can be no acceptance either. The awareness of being who you are can make you tremble.

In a relatively safe and comfortable way, we can gain the same experience by reading a novel or seeing a film or play. Many of the novels by Dutch writer Thomas Rosenboom, for example, show that we can even be ashamed of what a fictional character does in our stead. We recognize ourselves – against our will – in the literary characters. We see someone acting in a way that deters us, or perhaps even seems incomprehensible, and at the same time we identify with him or her. Sometimes we hope someone won't do what we nonetheless see him or her do. Literature, like psychiatric case studies, can reveal for a moment that we too are, in latent form, what we don't want to be, that we carry deep within ourselves that which repels us or that which we abhor.

However, this comparison with the literature may at the same time also point us to the way in which we can deal with it: a way that reconciles us at least to some extent, without relieving the tension. In a lecture, the Dutch writer Arnon Grunberg (2012) defines literature (or as he says, 'the story') as 'the description of one or more violations of the law', of 'violating taboos', of 'entering a forbidden place'. The characters commit that violation because they are stubborn, do not bow to the rules that organize our normal existence, or surrender to their passion. It does not always have to be done in the way of Sophocles' Antigone, who violates the laws of the state to do what the gods ask of her or her blood-tie demands of her; it is also possible in the way of Ivan Goncharov's character Oblomov, who indulges in his indolence and thereby violates the rule that one should make something of life; or in the way of Rosenboom's character Berend Bepol (in his novel *The New Man*) who, through his ambitious ideals, loses track of reality. Grunberg, who himself refers not only to *Antigone* but also to J.M. Coetzee's *Disgrace* and Joseph Roth's *Rebellion*, says: 'While power is maintained by the enforcement of faith in its taboos, literature derives its power from the desecration of what is considered to be holy outside this sanctuary. It can violate laws with impunity; it describes the violation of taboos.' According to Grunberg, it is important that the description of an offence does not necessarily glorify that offence. On the contrary: after all, the same story often shows that the offending character usually suffers from his offence.

However, the violation of the law or the taboo does show how precarious the power with which it is maintained is, whether it is the power of reality, of social conventions, or of the government that is at stake. However much that power presents itself as absolute, the actual violation shows how weak it is. As soon as its laws are ignored, power becomes something tragic or comical, according to Grunberg. This appears to be the case, for example, when, prompted by the offence, it persists and tries to maintain its power against all reason. Creon eventually puts his whole family in misery by holding on to the prohibition that was violated by Antigone. Even Oblomov has something 'heroic' in his disinterest for all activism in the world, and his opponent Stolz becomes increasingly boring because of his activism. Berend Bepol's attempts to break the power of the new man, Niesten, mainly lead to his own apocalyptic downfall.

Someone who defies power and transgresses the law does so because he or she does not believe in it; as Antigone obeys a higher law in her violation of the law of Creon. With it she follows something greater than herself, a higher power. The law of this higher power serves no practical purpose. The divine law that obliges Antigone to put everything at stake to bury her dead brother is unreasonable and incomprehensible. 'Antigone takes this (higher) unreasonableness seriously' and is therefore rightly called a fool by the choir, according to Grunberg. The behaviour of Oblomov and Bepol can only be called unwise or even foolish. The description of that foolishness shows how much the unreasonableness affects us – be it the power of the gods, ambition, fate or chance. It is the same unreasonableness as that which manifests itself in the uneasiness that we do not lose; no matter how much we organize our lives and our worlds according to criteria of usefulness and reasonableness.

Literature reminds us that even our rationality – in Grunberg's words – 'is built on an unreasonable basis'. Under our rationality lies the swamp of irrationality: the arbitrary, the incomprehensible, the furious, in short the divine. This memory can also be a kind of reconciliation. After all, we do not read literature to torment ourselves, even if we shudder when reading. Literature (and the same goes for the literary examples with which I opened this book in Chapter I.2, and *mutatis mutandis* for the other arts as well) makes us look at our lives in a way that at the same time does and does not distance ourselves from that life: we do not distance ourselves insofar as we identify with the characters, engage ourselves with their fate and sympathize with what they experience, but at the same time we do distance ourselves insofar as we keep at a distance that fate, which we recognize that it could also affect us – the distance between the stage and the spectator, the arm's length between book and reader.

Isn't this the therapeutic meaning of psychoanalysis, which I used as a guide in this section? After all, it does not claim to free the patient from his or her suffering and bring him or her happiness. What it does offer is a certain insight into suffering and therefore that second look.

The suggestion I would like to make is that this way in which art reconciles us with what at the same time remains unbearable can also offer a model for an ethical approach that focuses on the art of living well.

Such an approach should make room for this contemplative view of one's own life. It will not take away the tension from life, but it will make it a little more bearable. It does so by holding on to all our efforts to fulfil our desires in a reasonable and just way and complement it with a different view of our lives – one in which we face the futility and fragility of what we do and try. That second look does not take away the seriousness of the first, but allows us to laugh about it every now and then.

7 (Virtue) ethics and (the) art (of living well)

Does that have anything to do with Aristotelian virtue ethics, or should we now definitively leave that behind us, as we suspected at the beginning of this chapter? Of course the idea that there is no order in the world, no purpose in nature and no sense in existence creates an enormous distance between 'us' and Aristotle. Yet, in my opinion this does not mean an absolute break with his ethical design and the way in which it has been developed and expanded over its long history.

First, as has been said, the second look does not detract from the seriousness of the first. There is still nothing better that we can do than try to shape ourselves, that is to say our desires, as well as possible. Even if the world of those desires, which are formed by reason, is a fragile and precarious thing, without reasonable ground and always in danger of being disrupted, it still determines an important part of our lives, and we are likely to make this life better by transforming those desires into virtuous dispositions. The ethics of education, exercise and character building remains meaningful, even without the illusion that we could ever ensure happiness – an illusion that Aristotle himself did not have either.

Second, in the potentially reconciling effect of the contemplative view of one's own life, we can recognize something of the Stoic correction on Aristotelian ethics. The Stoics realized very well that our lives are ultimately not determined by our own insights and efforts, but by fate. Therefore, according to them, life is ultimately about becoming 'homologous' to that fate, to the all-encompassing nature. For the Stoics, that fate may represent the power of reason, but from the limited perspective of our small rationality we can hardly see it. Therefore, in this view there always remains an important difference between our moral efforts and the realization of the goal (happiness) to which they are directed. But for the Stoics, too, a person should nevertheless do what he or she can to ensure that he or she lives as he or she thinks is good. Only when it turns out that fate has something else in store for you does the highest virtue, in their opinion, consist in wanting exactly that thing. The Stoics will indeed relativize the conflict or the tension between their own efforts and homology with the great nature, because ultimately that great nature is reasonable and their own nature is part of it. Nevertheless, at the level of subjective experience, the difference is experienced as being full of tension. And the reconciling view of fate and nature is related to the contemplative view that art grants us.

Third, at this point we may even be able to recognize something of the addition of the Christian tradition to virtue ethics. The theological virtues are perfections that we do not control ourselves, and that, from a common-sense perspective, can only appear as follies. Isn't there a connection between the 'folly for the world' of faith, hope and love on the one hand, and the folly of the literary heroes I mentioned or of the absolute meaning that random persons or objects can acquire in a human life on the other hand? Of course there is first of all an important difference: the theological virtues are sanctioned by God and the reasonable order He represents, while the more or less pathological violations of the laws of normality show the fragility of that rationality and the abyss of absurdity beneath it. Nevertheless, the effect of faith in God's saving hand, on the one hand, and of the view of this horrifying absurdity, on the other, is too similar not to link them. The Christian addition to virtue ethics taught us that, in addition to the virtues by which we can perfect ourselves, there are also other virtues: those for which we can at best make ourselves receptive, but which are ultimately given to – or withheld from – us. Does psychoanalysis, as well as reading literature, perhaps offer a secular version of these theological virtues? Isn't the reconciling insight also something that you try to achieve, but without any guarantee of success?

Finally I return to Aristotle and Nietzsche once more. There is an extensive discussion in secondary literature about the question of what, according to Aristotle, happiness ultimately consists of. On the one hand, the construction and development of his ethics suggests that it is about a life that is optimally realizable in all respects: in the perfection of the intellectual faculties as well as in the perfection of the praxis of life within the community, the enjoyment of which is rewarded in the friendship with someone who has attained a similar degree of perfection. On the other hand, Aristotle states that the highest happiness is in the perfection of the highest activity, and that is the *theoria*, the understanding that he believes is most perfect when it relates to the principles of reality and to the most perfect movement in the cosmos: the movement of the heavenly bodies. My concern is not with the exegesis of Aristotle's text, but with whether and to what extent we can use his ethics to understand our own moral condition. If we take the concept less theoretically and instead relate it to human destiny, then the connection of both identifications of happiness is obvious. The highest achievement for a human being consists in the best possible praxis of life, supplemented by the awareness that this praxis is fragile: not so much because we are weak, but because the order within which we can be good, is itself without foundation.

I already referred to the (early) text in which Nietzsche compares the condition of the human being with that of someone sleeping on the back of a tiger. This tiger symbolizes the absence of a ground: the absurdity of existence, of which we should not have any knowledge in order to lead our lives. Nietzsche then goes on to outline two opposing ways of dealing with this condition, that of art and that of philosophy. Art produces a comforting illusion: the dream in which the sleeping person enjoys a happy and meaningful life. But philosophy seeks to unmask every illusion and tries to awaken the sleeper. 'Art', writes Nietzsche in *On the Pathos of Truth*, 'is more powerful than knowledge, because *it* desires life, whereas knowledge attains as its final goal – only annihilation' (PT, 66). Philosophy is thus – according to Nietzsche – a threat to life; that is to say: it would be, if it didn't fall asleep itself and merely dream about being awake and waking up others. Nietzsche had in mind a philosophy, a morality and a religion that intended to free people from their actual misery by sketching an image of a 'real' life in a 'true' world. However, he also sought the possibility of a different philosophy, a different way of thinking, one that does justice to the real world.

Life is an art. This art may require such a mindset: a way of thinking that does not lose itself in ideals, but that consists in the perhaps somewhat melancholic recognition that we are beings that are not perfect, so that 'true happiness' is not available to us, although that – fortunately – does not have to exclude moments of happiness. Such an approach is not opposed to art, but is capable of reconciling, as art does.

Literature

Appiah, Kwame Anthony (2008), *Experiments in Ethics*, Cambridge, MA: Harvard University Press.

Doris, John M. (1998), 'Persons, Situations and Virtue Ethics', *Noûs*, 32(4): 504–30.

Elsschot, Willem (1934), *Yesterday's Poems* (*Verzen van vroeger*), trans. Tanis Guest, Antwerpen: Willem Elsschot Genootschap.

Freud, Sigmund (1969–75), 'Das Unbehagen in der Kultur', in *Freud-Studienausgabe*, Vol. 9, 191–270, Frankfurt am Main: Fischer.

Goncharov, Ivan (2005), *Oblomov*, trans. David Magarshak, intro. Milton Ehre, London: Penguin.

Grunberg, Arnon (2012), 'Taboes van mensen en van goden', lecture given at the Leipziger Buchmesse, 'Das literarische Colloquium Berlin', 15 March.

Haidt, Jonathan and Craig, Joseph (2004), 'Intuitive Ethics: How Innately Prepared Intuitions Generate Culturally Variable Virtues', *Daedalus*, 133(4): 55–66.

Kant, I. (GMS) (1968), *Groundwork for the metaphysics of morals*, Translated by Allen W. Wood, New Haven: Yale University Press. (original: *Grundlegung zur Metaphysik der Sitten*. Darmstadt: Wissenschaftliche Buchgesellschaft 1968).

Kant, I. (MdS)(1996): *The Metaphysics of Morals*. Translated by Mary Gregor, Cambridge University Press (original: *Die Metaphysik der Sitten*. Darmstadt: Wissenschaftliche Buchgesellschaft 1975).

Montaigne, Michel de (1958), *Essays*, trans. J.M. Cohen, London: Penguin.

Moyaert, Paul (2011), 'Wat ons bindt aan een werkelijkheid die vereenzaamt. Hoe Lacan denkt over ethiek', *Ethische Perspectieven*, 21(1): 230–57.

Moyaert, Paul (2012), 'Antigone en hoe Lacan onze morele sensibiliteit begrijpt', *Psychoanalytische Perspectieven*, 30(1): 61–90.

Nietzsche, F. (AC) (1990) *The Antichrist*. In: Fr. Nietzsche, *Twilight of the Idols/ The Antichrist*, translated by R.J. Hollingdale, Penguin Books (original: *Der Antichrist*. In: KSA Vol. 6).

Nietzsche, F. (GD) (TI)(1990) *Twilight of the Idols* In: Fr. Nietzsche, *Twilight of the Idols/The Antichrist*, translated by R.J. Hollingdale, Penguin Books (original: *Götzendämmerung*. In: KSA Vol. 6).

Nietzsche, F. (GM) (1969), *On the Genealogy of Morals*. Translated by W. Kaufmann, New York: Vintage, (original: *Zur Genealogie der Moral*. In: KSA Vol. 5).

Nietzsche, F. (KSA) (1988), *Kritische Studienausgabe in 15 banden*, Berlin/ Munich: DTV.

Nietzsche, F. D: *Daybreak* Translated by R.J. Hollingdale, Cambridge University Press 1982 (original: *Morgenröthe*. In: KSA Vol. 3)..

Nietzsche, F. (HAH II.1 AOM)(1986) *Human, All Too Human*. Volume II, part 2 'Assorted Opinions and Maxims'. Translated by R.J. Hollingdale, Cambridge University Press (original: *Menschliches, Allzumenschliches*. II.2 'Vermischte Meinungen und Sprüche' In: KSA Vol. 2).

Nietzsche, F. (PT) (1979), 'On the Pathos of Truth', translated by Daniel Brezeale, in: Daniel Breazeale (ed.), *Philosophy and Truth*. New Jersey/London: Humanities Press Int., 61-66 (original: 'Über das Pathos der Wahrheit'. In: KSA 1 755-760.

Rosenboom, Thomas (2009), *De nieuwe man*, Amsterdam: Querido.

Tongeren, Paul van (1996), ' "A Splendid Failure": Nietzsche's Understanding of the Tragic', *Journal of Nietzsche Studies*, 11: 23–34.

Aphorisms

Odysseus

Some people always want to go elsewhere, others always want to go home. It's all about combining the two: not wandering around aimlessly but at the same time preventing you from finishing. Did Odysseus understand this art?

Traffic

In 'normal' traffic, we set off in order to get to (some)where we want to be. In our social lives, or social 'traffic', we are usually there either to figure out where it is we want to go, or despite the fact that we don't want to go anywhere.

Time

Time pulls our leg when we don't know how to use our legs.

Together

Even if we walk in silence and leave each other be, walking together is something completely different from walking by yourself, or walking the dog. The mere fact that someone else, another human being, is present changes the world. Whether he or she does something or not, whether he or she says something or not, that does not matter. His or her mere presence already dispels my indifference. The meaning that replaces it can be anything from irritation to pleasure, and from a challenge to boredom.

Walking

Being unhappy is being absent, says Kierkegaard in the words of Hegel. Not being at home where you are, not being present at the place and moment you are, not coinciding with yourself. Going for a walk can dispel this feeling of unhappiness, because it is a way to bring together the inner and outer world, your mind and your body. As soon as you start walking, your thoughts will take on the rhythm of your physical movement and this movement will become the vehicle of your thinking, reverie and feeling. The dynamics of inside and outside coincide.

Cycling

What one person experiences when walking, another may experience when running or cycling. Does this differ from person to person? Can cyclists think faster? Do fast thinkers like cycling more? Or is the faster movement aimed at something else? On silencing all thoughts and feelings? On exhausting the body to finally put the mind at rest?

Kinds of people

Some people are active and must therefore be in motion, others are peaceful and quiet, and must therefore be at rest to be themselves.

Alone

Someone who thinks is never alone. The 'solitary thinker' is at least two-sided. Sometimes he or she is even 'Legion' (Mk 5.9).

Sympathein

To empathize with another is to put oneself in someone else's position. If his or her feeling relates to you, however, this becomes problematic. Can I empathize with your fear of losing me? Suppose your love controls me, then my sympathy would continue the imprisonment; it would struggle with my desire for liberation. And what if I sympathize with your love for me? Isn't that vanity or narcissism? And yet, it does happen that a dying person mourns the suffering of his or her neighbours who mourn for his or her approaching death – he or she would die to free them from their suffering.

Giving oneself

Whoever gives him- or herself completely to his or her loved one has nothing left, not even him- or herself as the giver. Even love must be tempered.

Transference

Whoever thinks that love consists in fully surrendering to his or her loved one is in danger of falling in love with the one to whom he or she gives him- or herself completely. In psychoanalysis this is called 'transference'.

Knowing what you want

If you think that the good life is only a matter of knowing what you want, you probably don't know what that actually means: to will something.

Community

God and animals cannot doubt; humans can hardly do anything else, therefore we need others.